Bloody ~~W~~

John Williams was born in C̶a̶r̶d̶i̶f̶f̶. ~~He~~ ̶i̶s̶ ̶r̶o̶c̶k̶ critic for *GQ* magazine, and c̶o̶n̶t̶r̶i̶b̶u̶t̶e̶s̶ ̶t̶o̶ ̶t̶h̶e̶ *Independent, New Statesman, Ma̶r̶i̶e̶ ̶C̶l̶a̶i̶r̶e̶ and Arena*. His first book, *Into the Badlands* (available in Flamingo paperbacks), a highly acclaimed travelogue through contemporary American crime fiction, was published in 1991, and he is currently working on a novel. John Williams lives in north-west London with his family.

JOHN WILLIAMS

BLOODY VALENTINE

A Killing in Cardiff

HarperCollins*Publishers*

HarperCollins*Publishers*,
77–85 Fulham Palace Road,
Hammersmith, London W6 8JB.

A Paperback Original 1995
9 8 7 6 5 4 3 2 1

A catalogue record for this book is
available from the British Library

ISBN 0 00 638442 0
Set in Linotron Baskerville
by Rowland Phototypesetting Ltd
Bury St Edmunds, Suffolk

Printed and bound in Great Britain by
HarperCollinsManufacturing Glasgow

For my parents,
David and Gillie Williams,
with thanks

Contents

Acknowledgements

I would like to thank Malik Abdullahi and Lloyd Paris without whose determination there would have been no book, no defence campaign and three innocent men still serving a life sentence; and Alex Abdullahi for her hospitality and grace under enormous pressure.

Thanks also to Satish Sekar for his unselfishness with the results of his tireless research into the case, and to all those who agreed to be interviewed or otherwise helped with the information gathering; among them Leila Attfield, Stuart Hutton, Debbie Haggett, David Orton, Dan O'Neill, Keith Morell, Cyril, David Webster, Kermit, Jackie Harris.

I am grateful to Edward Morris for his friendship and hospitality during my stays in Cardiff; and to the friends who've helped me with advice and support, among them Robin Cook, Elizabeth Young, Martin Millar, Mike Oldfield, Stuart Home, Mike Hart, Sandhya Ellis and Jon Plumpton. And mostly thanks to my family: Charlotte, Henry and Owen.

Finally, thanks to Yusef Abdullahi, Stephen Miller and Tony Paris, victims of injustice.

Lynette White R.I.P.

Introduction

On 14 February 1988 the dead body of a twenty-year-old Cardiff prostitute, Lynette White, was discovered by her friend and colleague, Leanne Vilday in a semi-derelict flat above a bookie's in Butetown, Cardiff. She had been stabbed more than fifty times and had been lying there since the previous night.

In a way it was an ordinary murder, awful but ordinary. In another place and at another time it might have passed almost without comment, apart from the legacy of grief left to those who'd known her and whatever consequences God or justice may visit upon her killer.

But this murder didn't go away. Lynette White's death set in train events that were to change both the people who knew her and the neighbourhood in which she died, the place they once called Tiger Bay – events that have changed the world she lived in, almost beyond recognition.

This book is about what happened to Lynette White and about what happened to Butetown, what happened before and what happened after, and it's an attempt to explain why her death scarred so many lives.

ONE

The Lonesome Death of Lynette White

It was raining and she was in Despenser Gardens. Always seemed to rain in bloody Despenser Gardens. Three days she'd been back there. And she'd thought she'd never have to. Crichton Street was better. You could sit in the Custom House and have a warm and a laugh. Can of Breaker and a spliff, maybe get a line from Leanne if you're too knackered. Here there's just the Coldstream and she didn't even want to go in there in case she saw someone she knew. Saw her dad there once, first time he saw her working. He nearly died, the old bastard. Out on the piss with his mates, he had to pretend he didn't know. Of course he bloody knew. Do me a favour, he bloody knew all right.

Still, she was safe enough here. Stephen was too fucking stupid to figure out she'd be here. He'd be looking for her in the North Star. Maybe he'd go to the Custom House, but he wouldn't think of coming over here. And it was off fucking Francine's fucking family's turf too, thank Christ. Why she'd talk to the law about Francine she couldn't bloody imagine. Now she'd opened her big mouth and she was due in court to testify against Francine bloody Cordle. Nah, fucked if she was going to court to get into that kind of shit, stay out of the way for another week and she'd be all right.

Jesus, it was wet though. Maybe she could go round to Michael's on the Embankment, cup of tea and a spliff, maybe buy another ten-quid deal. Except she might see Nicola or one of them over there. Shit. Been out for two hours and made fifteen fucking quid. Wanked off a Paki in the alleyway, and then a blow job in an Astra. Christ, she could still taste him, mixed in with the chicken and chips. Oh, stop thinking about it and just do one more and then call it a night. Buy some cans and get blocked enough to sleep. Just a few more days and she'd get it sorted. Get it all sorted.

Second time this one's come by, looks like a student, looks like

I've seen him somewhere. God knows, I've seen enough of them before. Jesus, he looks nervous. You looking for business? Don't have a heart attack, for fuck's sake. Ten pounds outside, twenty pounds in, get out of this pissing rain. All right, inside is it, you've got a car have you?

In the cab she could see him better, floppy fringe and shaking like a leaf, older than she thought too, more like thirty-five than twenty, looked like a student but too old. Good looking, if you liked that sort of thing, which she didn't much, but something a bit, a bit, a bit like a young person with an old person's eyes or an old person with a young person's eyes. Something kind of off anyway, but what the fuck, twenty quid and hustlers can't be choosers. Valentine's tomorrow too. Stephen had wanted to take her to see his mother. So he said anyway. But what she was going to do with him she didn't know. She'd had enough of it. No fucking respect, like Paul said.

Out of the car at James Street. Christ, the place looked worse every time she saw it. Front door practically fell open. Up the stairs into the flat. Follow me into the front, love, the electric's off but it's lighter there. Sit on the bed, take your shoes off, that's twenty quid then, ta, luv. Put that on now, which way do you want . . .

Which was when she saw the knife and she knew it was over, knew before she screamed that the fucking little ferret-face queer from upstairs wouldn't help, knew her daddy couldn't help, knew her mam couldn't help, knew no one would fucking help. Knew Stephen couldn't help and she knew that she'd loved him and she'd loved Mark and she'd loved them all and she'd loved all the black boys she'd let have her all those times, and she knew she'd never have a baby now.

And then he was killing her. He killed her quickly because he loved her too and he was so angry and upset the way she'd behaved to him. How could she do that? How could she say those things? He tried to cut her head off with one swinging smash of the knife and her throat just came apart and he knew she was dead and he just fell on her, started stabbing her breasts and stabbing and stabbing and, oh sweet Jesus, oh that hurt, he must have hit her bone with the knife and his hand slipped and he cut himself, cut his hand. Really deep, oh god, it hurt, and just now he really lost it, now he'd really killed the fucking bitch.

And five minutes later he saw what he had done and knew that he'd come in his pants and he got out of there and he was glad that it was late and it was dark and he was surprised that when he walked out of there no one was waiting for him. But as he walked to his car he thought, it's all right. No one fucking cares.

Leanne had brought three Pakis back to the flat. She did two of them herself but then the baby started crying and she had to get Angela to do the third. And then in the middle of all this shit in came Maria, Paulie's missus, and she was screaming bloody murder about little Craig not being for Paulie and Leanne told her to shut her fucking mouth 'cause he's my boy's father and then Maria chased her into the bathroom and hit her in the eye with her red, white and blue umbrella and there was blood all over the place.

And when all that shit finished and Maria and the punters left, Leanne had a black eye and bruises all over her face and Angela says you're not going out looking like that but Leanne does another line of speed and says fucking hell I am, I'm going over the North Star for a drink. And Angela goes oh I'm looking after Craig, am I? and Leanne says I fucking pays you, don't I, and out she goes.

But before she gets to the North Star she looks up at her flat over the bookie's, sees the front door open and the speed kicks in and says what's happening here then, why not see if Lynette's there, see if she's all right. And in she goes and pushes the flat door open which you don't have to be fucking Frank Bruno to manage and blocked as she is she knows it, she smells it before she sees it, but maybe it's the speed that stops her from being sick. Though when the little queer came down he went white fast enough and ran back up looking as sick as a dog. But the speed just said get out of here. Get fucking out of here, you don't want anything to do with this, oh Jesus, it's my flat. Oh Jesus, Lynette's dead in my fucking flat.

And she runs back over the road and gets Angela and they try to move the body, try to take her outside but that's a stupid idea, she's just too fucking heavy. So she just told the queer to shut his mouth and went back to Angela's and she felt like she was going crazy, so she went over to the North Star. And she was just in time, half past three, Ronnie was there and thank Christ for that. So she went back to his sister's

13

but she couldn't shake it, she kept talking about Lynette like a silly cow. And at 6.30 she couldn't stand it and told him she was going home. He couldn't care.

TWO

The Legend of Tiger Bay

Tiger Bay was the original pirate town. The way I heard it
as a child, the real old-time pirates, Captain Morgan and his
crew, used this promontory off the then small town of Cardiff
as a base: a little piece of Britain that was beyond the law.
God knows if it's true or whether my addled memory has
simply cobbled together a new myth out of two or three old
ones, but still, it's a legend that suits the wild side of the
Welsh.

What we know for sure is that Butetown, not yet Tiger
Bay, came out of the Industrial Revolution: in the 1840s the
Marquis of Bute ran a railway from the new mines of the
south Wales valleys to the Bristol Channel, coming out at
Cardiff, by the mouth of the River Taff. Huge new docks were
built at the end of the promontory, and the nascent city spread
south to meet them. They called this settlement between the
docks and the town Butetown, after the man whose coffers it
was filling. And from the beginning the arrangement of railway
lines, Bristol channel and river was such that there was a
natural division between Butetown and the rest of Cardiff.

In those early days, though, Butetown was the heart of
Cardiff. Mount Stuart Square, at the entrance to the docks,
was the city's commercial hub and Loudoun Square, in the
heart of Butetown, was among the city's smartest addresses,
boasting a Young Ladies' Seminary as well as providing a
home for the shipwrights, builders, master mariners and
merchants, the new aristocrats of a seafaring city.

The second half of the nineteenth century saw Cardiff
expand at a breathtaking rate. By the end of the century it was
one of the world's biggest, busiest ports. The sheer numbers of

ordinary seamen using the port forced changes in the area's make-up. The smart houses of Loudoun Square were converted into seamen's lodging houses, the merchant classes retreated into the main body of the city which soon sprouted smart northern suburbs, and the seafaring supremos, the ships' captains and so on, congregated around the southern tip of the island, in smart streets like Windsor Esplanade.

By now Butetown was home to a fair cross-section of the world's seafaring peoples – Chinese, Lascars, Levantines, Norwegians, Maltese, Spaniards and all. A wild and licentious community was emerging, finding worldwide fame as 'Tiger Bay'. Black seamen too, both from East Africa and the West Indies, were a part of this cosmopolitan mix, the first of them arriving as early as 1870, and by 1881 being numerous enough to have their own Seamen's Rest. By the time of the beginning of the First World War, there were around seven hundred coloured seamen in Cardiff, though this was still a mostly transient population of men without families.

The war changed everything. Many of Tiger Bay's citizens joined the war effort. Seamen went into the Navy and Merchant Navy. The *Western Mail* reported, in 1919, that fourteen hundred black seamen from Cardiff lost their lives in the war (which also demonstrates the somewhat unreliable nature of the era's statistics – there having allegedly been only seven hundred black people in Cardiff). Others joined the Army, the West Indian regiments or the Cardiff City Battalion. A Mr Rees recalled, in the *South Wales Echo*, that: 'All the boys of military age joined up and most of them paid the penalty, some at the Dardanelles, and a lot with the Cardiff City Battalion at Mametz Wood.'

Conscription into the Army also left a huge gap in the domestic labour force and, at the same time, East African trading ships were being requisitioned for the Navy, thus leaving a pool of unemployed sailors. So in Cardiff, as also happened in Liverpool, factory jobs were opened up to the seamen. Unsurprisingly, now that they were based in Cardiff for a substantial period of time, the sailors began to put down roots and to make the first moves towards an integration into the wider community – one aspect of which was the forging of relationships with local women. This last development fore-shadowed the GI bride phenomenon of the Second World War, except for the crucial distinction that this time the exotic suitors were not intending to whisk their brides across the ocean, but were planning to stay put in Butetown.

Trouble came with the war's end. The soldiers returned, unemployment loomed. Black workers were thrown out of their factory jobs, and seafaring work was likewise in high demand. Black unemployment rapidly became chronic and meanwhile general white unemployment became one of the key issues of the day. In some cities, notably Glasgow where John MacLean, 'the British Lenin', held sway, the whiff of communist revolution was in the air, and the government was briefly terrified. In sea-faring cities like Cardiff and Liverpool, however, the racial minority was fitted up for the role of scapegoat.

Racial tensions first began to appear amongst the returning soldiers. Peter Fryer in his remarkable and ground-breaking history of the black presence in Britain, *Staying Power*, tells the awful tale of an incident in a veterans' hospital in Liverpool in which five hundred white soldiers set upon the fifty black inmates, many of whom were missing at least one limb. A pitched battle was fought with crutches and walking sticks as the principal weapons (though not all the white soldiers sided with the racists: a contemporary account, in the *African Tele-graph*, records that 'When the [military police] arrived on the scene to restore order, there were many white soldiers seen standing over crippled black limbless soldiers, and protecting them with their sticks and crutches from the furious onslaught of the other white soldiers until order was restored.').

If the Belmont Hospital affair had an element of cruel farce, much of what followed was tragic. In the summer of 1919, in South Shields and Liverpool and Cardiff, Britain's first race riots of the modern era broke out. The post-war slump pro-vided the conditions for these mass outbreaks of racist violence

– and Fryer clearly demonstrates that these riots consisted of white mobs randomly attacking blacks – but it was generally sex that provided the flash point. The returning troops could easily be goaded into believing that 'their' women were being stolen. Whites would repeatedly claim, as justification for assault, that blacks had been 'making suggestive remarks to our women' or some such. And the newspapers were swift to follow this line. Fryer records a *Liverpool Courier* editorial pontificating that:

> One of the chief reasons of popular anger behind the present disturbances lies in the fact that the average negro is nearer the animal than is the average white man, and that there are women in Liverpool who have no self-respect.

The 1919 race riots were not simply regrettable occurrences from far-off days but rather the crucible in which Britain's subsequent racial pathology was formed. The cry for tribal solidarity to protect their jobs from these 'outsiders' was overlaid with sexual hysteria: not simply 'they're taking our women' but 'they're taking our women because they're sex-beasts'. This hysteria presumably arose from a combination of black people having long been caricatured as apelike or bestial, and the legacy of Victorian prudery that regarded sex as a bestial activity. Certainly what emerged was the potent construction of blackness as both an economic and a sexual threat.

According to Fryer the flash point of the Cardiff riot on 11 June 1919 was, ironically enough, 'A brake containing black men and their white wives, returning from an excursion, attracted a large and hostile crowd'. However, a recently unearthed account, written by a policeman present at the time, gives a rather less genteel and more detailed account. According to PC Albert Allen (as reprinted in the *South Wales Echo*):

> I was the only PC on duty at the Wharf when it started and I was on duty the whole time it lasted in the Docks area. First

of all I would like to point out the cause. In Cardiff there were quite a number of prostitutes and quite a number of pimps who lived on their earnings. When conscription came into force these pimps were called up. Then a number of prostitutes went to the Docks district and lived with these coloured people who treated them very well. When the war finished the pimps found their source of income gone as the prostitutes refused to go back to them. The night the trouble started, about 8.30 p.m., a person who I knew told me to expect some trouble. I asked him why and he explained that the coloured men had taken the prostitutes on an outing to Newport in two horse wagons and that a number of pimps were waiting for their return.

Next, by Allen's account, the pimps attacked the wagons near the Monument – at the edge of the city centre and fifty yards or so from the Bute Street bridge which signals the beginning of Butetown – and a pitched battle ensued before police reinforcements dispersed the crowd and attempted to cordon off Butetown. What was by now an angry white mob, among them many armed demobilized soldiers, then proceeded to rampage around the town looking for blacks to assault. Some managed to get past the police lines and into Butetown, where they smashed the windows of Arab boarding houses.

This initial disturbance petered out around midnight, but the rioting was to continue for several more days. On the second day a Somali boarding house in the centre of town was burnt down and its inhabitants badly beaten. More boarding houses were then burnt down in Bute Street, and an Arab beaten to death. On the third day a white mob gathered once more in the centre of town and prepared for another assault on Butetown.

This time, however, Butetown was ready for them. If its position on an isthmus at the bottom of the city made Butetown a convenient ghetto, it also made it a fortress. There was only one easy way in from the town centre, via Bute Street itself, and the other approaches, from East Moors and Grangetown, could be easily watched, so armed sentries were posted – the blacks too having brought their weapons home from the war – and the community waited. As a *South Wales News* reporter saw it on 14 June 1919:

> The coloured men, while calm and collected, were well prepared for any attack, and had the mob from the city broken through the police cordon there would have been bloodshed on a big scale ... Hundreds of negroes were collected, but these were very peaceful, and were amicably discussing the situation amongst themselves. Nevertheless, they were in a determined mood and ready to defend 'our quarter of the city' at all costs ... Long-term black residents said: It will be hell let loose if the mob comes into our streets ... if we are unprotected from hooligan rioters who can blame us for trying to protect ourselves?'

Their defence was successful and the rioting died away over the next few days, leaving in its wake three dead and many more injured, but a decisive corner had been turned. The authorities' only response to the troubles was to offer to repatriate the black community. Around six hundred black men took up the offer within the next few months, though many of the returning West Indians went back with the express intention of inciting anti-British feeling. And, indeed, within days of some of the Cardiff seamen returning to Trinidad, fighting against white sailors broke out, followed by a major dock strike.

The majority, however, decided to stay on, to make a permanent home on this ground they'd fought for. But from this point on Butetown was not simply a conventional ghetto or a colourful adjunct to the city's maritime life, but effectively an island. It was not simply a black island: the area had always had a white Welsh population and continued to do so, there was an Irish presence too as well as Chinese, Arab and European sailors, and refugees from successive European conflicts as well. And as the black or coloured population was initially almost exclusively male, Butetown rapidly became a predominantly mixed-race community, almost unique in Britain, the New Orleans of the Taff delta, home of the creole Celts. But this integration was firmly confined to Tiger Bay: above the Bute bridge you were back in the same hidebound old Britain.

The following twenty years before the next great war did nothing but further entrench the racial segregation. What soon became known as 'the colour bar' came down to deal with black immigration. Industry was almost entirely closed to blacks and seafaring jobs were made ever harder to obtain by cynical manipulation of nationality laws. In Cardiff the police arbitrarily interpreted the Aliens Order of 1920 to mean that any coloured person was *de facto* an alien. If they produced a British passport to prove otherwise that would simply be seized and thrown away. And, as if times were not hard enough already, the slump of 1929 simply saw economic matters go from bad to worse.

So, trapped as they were between the bigots and the murky green sea, the people of Butetown had to construct their own economy, based on catering to the traditional desires of men who have spent the last few months on the ocean wave. The community that emerged, though economically deprived and rife with disease, was possessed of a vitality that is remembered with great fondness by virtually all those who lived there in the inter-war period. Harold Fowler was born in Butetown in 1905, the son of a West Indian seaman and a Welsh ship captain's daughter. Talking to the *South Wales Echo* in 1970 he recalled that 'Bute Road used to be like St Mary Street. It had jewellers' shops, restaurants, big poultry stores, laundries, music shops . . . There was always lots of music in Tiger Bay. The sailors and the prostitutes used to drink and dance in the pubs and cafés. And there was Louis Facitto's barber shop. He had an automatic piano with bells and drums attached to it. You put a penny in and it played to you.'

Noise, though, was always one of the community's defining characteristics. Mrs Bahia Johnson remembers in her unpublished memoir of living in Tiger Bay in the thirties, 'On almost every door there were cages with screaming parrots and cockatoos. Were they able to talk! Believe me they put many a seaman's language in the shade. Many people were forbidden to put them outside their homes. Tiny canaries sang in their little cages. There were men with little monkeys on their shoulders. They wore little red hats and gloves. Often a barrel organ would be wheeled around the streets with a little monkey on top. In the Roaring Twenties Bute Street was like a Persian market . . .'

Tiger Bay's landmarks were its pubs. Eleven of them crammed into the neighbourhood: The Freemason's Arms (better known to one and all as the Bucket of Blood), the Rothesay Castle (or House of Blazes), the Adelphi Hotel, the Loudoun Hotel, the Glamorgan Hotel, the Bute Tavern, the Peel Hotel, the Cardigan Hotel, the Bute Castle Hotel, the Marchioness of Bute and the Westgate Hotel.

Wally Towner, long-time landlord of the Freemason's, admitted that its nickname was not undeserved:

We had some tough times down there all right. It was nothing for a couple of pounds' worth of glasses to go in one night. I had a shillelagh behind the bar and I used to use it now and then. There was a big coloured girl there. She could knock a man out and would think nothing of it. She came to my rescue many times. One night there was a brawl in the smoke room. One chap was out on the floor. She'd given him one. I got a siphon and squirted it in his face.

That was a general occurrence. If they fought in the pub you just had to wade in and take a chance. Once one of the prostitutes saved my life. She took off her stiletto shoe and hit them over the head while I got up. There were the girls there of course. They lived for the day, they would make a lot of money and live it up, but some mornings they'd come in with black eyes, the pimps had given them those if they hadn't made enough.

The girls used to quarrel sometimes. One day I saw some of them fighting, clawing at each other. I put two in the gents' toilet, two in the ladies' toilet and I told them not to come out till they'd finished scrapping. 'I'll give a bottle of wine to the winner,' I said. My pub was a great one for the vino, 6d a glass.

22

The police were marvellous down there. They didn't always lock them up. They just used to take them round the back and give them a damn good hiding. They can't do that today, poor fellows. And of course the boys used to come down from the valleys to see the place and see the girls. They were looking for trouble.

One of those Valleys boys, 'Charlie' as he called himself in the *Echo*, remembers his first visits to Tiger Bay:

I went down there first because it was such a contrast with my home town of Merthyr. Merthyr was very drab at the time. It was a distressed area. I joined the army in 1926 to get away from the place and they sent me to Maindy Barracks in Cardiff. On our nights out the more adventurous of us dodged the military police and went down Tiger Bay. There were honky-tonks from one end of Bute Street to the other. It was great, so gay and colourful. We were 'seeing life', as we called it. We went in the back rooms and danced with the girls . . .

The inevitable happened. I got caught and had a dose of detention. When I came out I decided to join with some of the real boys of the bay. I thought, 'This is the life for me,' and I sold my uniform to a docker. So I'd burned my boats good and proper. [A career in petty crime ensued until] two of us got caught in a tobacconist's shop in Pontypridd and were remanded to await trial at the assizes. The girls visited us with cigarettes and tobacco. I got three months and naturally returned to my friends in the Bay. I was met at the nick gate and given a few bob and a good booze-up in the Freemason's, the haunt of pimps, prostitutes, wide boys and queers.

But, like Wally Towner, Charlie had scarcely a bad word to say for the police of the time: 'There was a comradeship. They were out to get us and we were out to get them. We had very great respect for each other. In those days we believed that if a copper and another fellow were having a go, let them have a go. But if three or four boys were beating up a policeman we'd go to his aid. And if three or four cops set on one man, we'd help him.'

And it's the same story from old-time Bay cops like William Rees, who started out as a Tiger Bay copper in 1921, stayed there till 1941, and finally retired as Chief Constable of Stockport. 'I made more friends down there than anywhere else, real genuine friends,' he recalls. 'The great thing was knowing how to speak to them. If you spoke officiously you could expect trouble. But if you treated them like a pal you got your evidence. Of course there was trouble now and then, but there was far more violence in other parts of Cardiff, such as Caroline Street and Wood Street.'

Butetown even had more flamboyant cops than the rest of Cardiff. Mr Rees remembers a detective called Gerry Broben: 'He was a famous figure in his khaki breeches, leggings and trilby hat. And he always had a pipe. He used to walk around in uniform with a pipe in his mouth. Time was of no consequence to him. He used to roll up at half past ten or eleven in the morning but nobody knew when he went off duty. Maybe two or three in the morning. He was a fount of information. He always knew where to get it. He was always behind the curtains, so to speak.'

Butetown's most celebrated curtains were those of the Chinese community. 'From 190 to 198 Bute Street was all Chinese houses,' recalls Harold Fowler. 'The Chinese were great gamblers – and many of them used to travel down from their laundries in the Valleys to Tiger Bay to play paka pu, a kind of lottery game with numbers, and fan tan, played with shells.

'At the back of one or two of those houses were opium dens. There used to be bunks in those rooms with curtains around them. In the middle of the room was a small table with a lamp and several opium pipes. A man sitting at the table would put a ball in the pipe and light it for them and then they used to lie down on a bunk and dream their dreams.'

Well respected though the police may have been, it was within the community that the real arbiters of right and wrong were found. Community leaders of real authority emerged. Chief among them were a West Indian boarding-house master called John Purvo, who became the local president of the Negro Universal Improvement Association, and Peter Link, known as 'the King of the Africans', another boarding-house master and a man noted for his diligence in fighting for the rights of black seamen.

In the late 1930s Tiger Bay was graced with the presence of a more celebrated black leader: Paul Robeson, the great American singer, actor and communist who came to Britain to appear in two films – Hollywood of course having little use for black men at the time, except as eyeball-rolling Stepin Fetchits – *The Proud Valley* and *Sanders of the River*. Butetown actor/writer Neil Sinclair recently contributed a fascinating memoir of Tiger Bay and the movies to an excellent series of 'Bay Originals' newspapers published by Fullemploy Wales; he remembers that 'Robeson found a welcome in Tiger Bay, where he made several visits to the Jason home on the west side of Loudoun Square. There he used to visit the African-American activist Aaron Mossell who lodged there.'

The film that brought Robeson to South Wales was *The Proud Valley*, a charming if unsurprisingly sentimental tale of a black seaman landing up in a Valleys mining village, overcoming prejudice to become a stalwart of the choir (Robeson remains an enduring favourite with the still mighty choirs of the Valleys) and ending up with the immortal line 'we're all black down the pit'.

Robeson was the only black face in *The Proud Valley*, but *Sanders of the River* called for two hundred and fifty black extras, and Tiger Bay provided many of them – including among them, remarkably enough, the future Kenyan revolutionary leader Jomo Kenyatta, then a penniless anthropology student living in London. Sinclair recalls, 'Everyone knew the witch-doctor dancing wildly in the African village was Mr Graham from Sophia Street. And that was Uncle Willy Needham in the loincloth that he kept for years after. The little black baby Robeson held in his arms was Deara Williams. Deara went on to become an exotic dancer with an act including a boa

25

constrictor. And we all waited for the "River Boat Song" to begin so we could all join in. "Iyee a ko, I yi ge de," we would chant in unison with Paul and all the African boatmen. Some twenty years later you could often see a gang of Bay boys on a separated timber log, singing the "River Boat Song", rowing across the lake of the timber float, a little south of west Canal Wharf.'

And then there was another great upheaval. The Second World War rolled around and once again black faces were grudgingly invited into the factories. Meanwhile Tiger Bay's reputation was such that black American GIs would converge on Cardiff from all over Britain when they had some leave. So throughout the hostilities it was business as usual in the world of illicit leisure.

After the war, the decline of the shipping industry was a devastating blow to the community. It deprived residents of both seafaring jobs and the money brought in by visiting sailors. But still, for a while Butetown continued to flourish. Mass immigration from the West Indies began, and at first Cardiff was one of the major destinations, a place where new-comers could be sure of a friendly welcome – to this day Cardiff remains a haven for Somali refugees.

In the fifties a new arrival could stroll down Bute Street and find, in rapid succession, the Cuban Café, the Ghana Club, Seng Lee's Laundry, the Somali People's restaurant and Hamed Hamed's grocers. The House of Blazes and the Bucket of Blood were still open for business. And, for a place to stay, there was, for instance, the Cairo Hotel, run by Arab ex-seaman Ali Salaiman and his wife Olive, a valleys Methodist who converted to Islam and whose five daughters, in true Butetown style, married an Arab, a Welshman, a Maltese, an Englishman and a Dutch Muslim.

One of the new arrivals was a young Trinidadian called Michael de Freitas, who was later to achieve brief fame as Britain's apostle of Black Power, Michael X, and later still was to be hanged for murder, back home in Trinidad, under the name of Michael Abdul Malik. His autobiography, published

in 1968, is unsurprisingly self-justifying and generally econ-
omical with the truth but it contains this fond reminiscence
of life in Tiger Bay in the fifties:

The Bay was a world of its own, cut off from the rest of the
city. A black world. It swarmed with West Indians, Arabs,
Somalis, Pakistanis and a legion of half-caste children. In its
food stores you could buy cassavas and red peppers and in the
restaurants you could eat curries and rice dishes just like those
in the West Indies.

The city's black people, who mostly worked in the docks,
were the sweetest people I've ever met in Britain. They had a
real friendliness. Everyone seemed to be married to everyone
else's sister and they'd all sit on the doorsteps of their elegant,
dilapidated old houses chatting and exchanging greetings . . .
I usually lived with a half-caste family who cooked Trinidadian
food and I would spend my time talking, going to the Friday
night dance at the solitary dance hall, and watching the street
gambling. This was illegal, of course, but even the policemen
had grown up in Tiger Bay, and when they saw a crowd standing in a circle they'd know a couple of men were in the middle
shooting dice and they'd stroll in the other direction. They
very rarely broke up a game.

There were a lot of old timers, old sea salts, in the Bay and
when I sat around chatting with them they'd always tell me
the same thing – to stay with the Norwegians and not get
mixed up with British ships because there was no future on
them for a black man; he couldn't get anywhere.

For much the same reason they seldom crossed the canal
which formed a frontier between Tiger Bay and the rest of
Cardiff. They preferred to stay in the family atmosphere away
from the cold prejudice they met in the white world beyond
. . . Like many other black people from Tiger Bay I've had
the experience of going up into the white town, standing in a
bar and calling for a half pint and having the barman look
straight through me and serve everyone else until there was
nothing to do but leave.

Not that white people ever left Tiger Bay alone. They were
always driving across the canal bridge at night and slumming
it along Bute Street. They had the idea that the Bay was a

den of vice and violence and they wanted to add a little spice to their lives.

I don't think I ever saw a fight in Tiger Bay. All I remember are the smiling families on the doorsteps and the beautiful black children playing everywhere.

By the late fifties slum clearance was the watchword in town planning, and Butetown was sure enough a slum, with its TB rate seven times that of the rest of the city. In 1957 the South African External Affairs Minister, Eric Louw, used Butetown as an example of British hypocrisy in their condemnation of apartheid, proclaiming it to be a ghetto worse than any to be found in Cape Town. In response the radical South African priest Trevor Huddleston visited Butetown and found it to be a slum indeed but racially speaking 'a wonderful community'.

Plans were drawn up for Butetown's redevelopment and Tiger Bay enjoyed a first flush of celebrity even as it was under sentence of extinction. A film called *Tiger Bay* was made, directed by J. Lee Thompson and based on the Howard Spring novel set around the turn of the century, with Hayley Mills as the plucky heroine. The filmmakers, however, took one look at the real Tiger Bay and opted to shoot most of the film in the genteel Edwardian seaside resort of Penarth instead. The real Tiger Bay did provide a host of extras and bit-part actors, though, among them Neil Sinclair. He recalls in his 'Bay Original' article, 'I was the boy that fought with Hayley in the film and prevented her from playing with us down at the Pier head. "Get back to London, Gilly Evans. You don't belong here!" I said. *Tiger Bay* is loved by the local inhabitants not so much for its story, although it is quite enthralling, but for its scenery. Everyone knew that Herbert Street was not actually in Tiger Bay but we still thrill to see our Junie Fettah calypsoing down that street in the wedding celebration, to the strains of "Never Make a Pretty Woman Your Wife".'

Meanwhile the real Tiger Bay gave its most celebrated protégée to the world – the most histrionic of UK chanteuses, Miss Shirley Bassey. No matter that Bassey was not strictly speaking from the Docks at all, but another less romantically named neighbourhood, she made her name there and 'the girl from Tiger Bay' had a rather better ring to it than 'the superstar from Splott'!

And then the axe came down. In the sixties virtually all of the old Tiger Bay, the central portion of Butetown, was torn down and replaced with a combination of high- and low-rise council housing, leavened with a new community centre and a new mosque. Meanwhile Cardiff had dwindled to nothing as a port, and Butetown residents of whatever colour were lucky to get the most menial of jobs, faced as they were with blanket discrimination (as detailed by Dilip Hiro in his 1967 report for *New Society*). The community was henceforth simply ignored by the rest of the city, with just a couple of clubs left to attract the occasional intrepid outsider. When the *Echo* published its 1970 tribute to Tiger Bay all the interviewees seemed to take it for granted that an era was over. Betty Anderson, of the Adelphi, was typical in her lament: 'There's no Tiger Bay now. The Tiger's dead. The life has gone, hasn't it.' As was Harold Fowler when he said, 'It was alive. It's gone, never to return, but it brings back memories. There used to be dancing and jollification. People made their own amusement then. Today they watch television. You can go down there now and it's like going into an estate like Llanrumney.' Mr Fowler was one of the many docks people who were moved to the new estates of Llanrumney and Llanederyn following the redevelopment.

But still there would be the occasional public reminder of times gone by. Butetown had always been known for its funerals – most celebrated of all being that of peerless Jim Driscoll, the legendary Cardiff boxer, with a mile-long procession and a model boxing ring on top of the coffin. And all the stops were pulled out one more time for the 1978 funeral of Vic Parker, the Bay's very own legendary blues guitarist, who was given a full New Orleans marching band send-off.

Butetown's decline ran slowly on into the eighties. The depleted community quietly endured massive unemployment, apparently cut off from the rest of the world, barely flickering during the riots of 1981, evolving a Welsh creole community out of time and out of town, noticed only when it came to the annual carnival and secure at least in the knowledge that it had little else to lose.

At least not until the prospect of Docklands redevelopment, long a rumour, at last became a reality.

I was born little more than a mile from Butetown. The foundry and factory that my great-great-grandfather founded and my father worked in when I was a child were, given an unusually good arm, a stone's throw from Butetown. One of our neighbours, in the village outside Cardiff where I grew up, worked in the Docks. Yet in the first sixteen years of my life I remember going through – not stopping in, just passing through – Butetown maybe three times. So far as the regular life of the city went, it was convenient to act as if Butetown did not exist. Respectable folk didn't venture there much and Butetown folk were tacitly expected not to show up elsewhere too often. Certainly, there were far fewer black faces in town when I was growing up than there are today.

Growing up, I saw the Cardiff my parents knew. And though they were both born and bred in the city, theirs was a city within a city, sharing the same centre but radiating to the north and west rather than the south and east, and made up of toney neighbourhoods like Cyncoed, where I spent the first couple of years of my life, or semi-rural Lisvane, where my father's mother lived.

Once I was seventeen and living, away from my parents, in Cardiff itself, in flats in Splott and Riverside and Cathays, the Cardiff I knew changed. One night, going to see a band called the Young Marble Giants in a place called the Casablanca Club in Butetown, I had to ask the bus driver where to get off and rely on a helpful fellow passenger to show me the club. I had precious little idea where I was.

In the 1970s, a time when the British caste system was a lot less rigid than in my parents' day, it was hardly unusual for a middle-class kid like me to live in a crumbling flat in Splott and hang out in Grassroots punk coffee bar, playing guitar with a terrible post-punk band and going down the Docks for a dole-cheque big night out. But even then Butetown was marginal to the life of the city. People may have been more or less dimly aware that there were some clubs down the bottom there and there were still prostitutes hanging out around the Custom House at the top end, but, in general, if Butetown was referred to at all, it was in the past tense. What replaced the real Butetown in the mind of the city was the newly minted legend of 'Tiger Bay'.

'Tiger Bay' was a wonderful, vibrant but vanished place that had now to be spoken of in the terms you'd apply to a reprobate uncle now sadly deceased, to be wondered at in tones of faintly scandalized affection. Lamentably this 'Tiger Bay' was no more, had disappeared in the sixties, when the old streets had been torn down and replaced by the tower blocks of today. The fact that there were still people living there, that they didn't disappear with the quaint old slums, was simply inconvenient. By rights they should have just been carted away with the bulldozers or transplanted to Llanederyn or Ely where they could be entirely forgotten. Remaining in Butetown, just a few hundred yards from the city centre, was a little inconsiderate but nothing the average Cardiffian couldn't learn to ignore.

Of course Butetown wasn't the only Cardiff neighbourhood to undergo sweeping changes over the past thirty years. The city centre too is now massively changed from the way it was when I was growing up in the sixties. Then there were two main shopping streets, Queen Street and St Mary Street, running at right angles to each other away from Cardiff Castle (the Marquis of Bute's extraordinary mock-medieval folly that dominates the town – surely the ultimate act of *nouveau riche* power, to build your own baronial home with coal mining millions). Each of these streets had elegant covered Victorian shopping arcades criss-crossing them, and a sprinkling of more or less grand department stores.

All this remains today, and St Mary Street and its arcades, in particular, make up a really splendid Victorian shop-perama. But the hinterland, the space enclosed by the two main streets, has been greatly altered. This used to be full of various seedy little back streets, with their run-down cafés, dubious book stores and down-and-out boozers, Frederick Street, Bridge Street and the rest. All gone. They've been replaced by a bloody great brand new eighties edifice, the St David's Centre, an absolutely typical where-the-hell-am-I, is this Swindon or Seattle, generic shopping mall. Ringing the mall are the inevitable car parks plus a couple of sops to the public good: a new library, the St David's Hall, where Tom Jones can be seen this year and every other year until the end of time, and the National Ice Rink which hosts Cardiff's all-conquering ice hockey team. Oh, and right on the top of the Salutation, the world's gloomiest – and for while my favourite – pub, there's a Toys R Us.

I remember the beginnings of the city's facelift. When I was around nine years old a shop front appeared on St Mary Street, emblazoned with the words 'Centreplan 70' and inside was a huge model of a massive planned redevelopment of the city centre. Myself I thought it looked wonderful. Progress still looked like a good thing to a pre-teen the year after man landed on the moon, and the more Cardiff might come to resemble Gotham City the better, as far as I was concerned. I loved Centreplan 70 and used to drag my mother repeatedly back to look at the model and exercise my small influence on this utopian development, for we the general public were invited to suggest names for the new streets in this, the best of all possible cities. So I was engaged in heavy lobbying for my hero of the moment, Cardiff City centre forward John 'Good with his Head' Toshack.

By 1971, though, John Toshack had been sold to Liverpool for £110,000 (but had not yet published his seminal volume of poetry *Gosh It's Tosh*), Cardiff had missed promotion to the First Division by a single point and Centreplan 70 was well on the way to its eventual oblivion. The following decade saw little more than a steady decline in the fortunes of South Wales.

Which is why I found it hard not to be somewhat sceptical when I first heard news of the Cardiff Bay Development. First I heard was, I think, when I was drinking in the most beautiful of the Docks pubs, the Mount Stuart, a wonderful sprawling Victorian boozer. The rumour was that it was imminently going to be knocked down to make way for the flyover that would form part of the ring road round the south of Cardiff. Seven or eight years later there's still a space where the Mount Stuart was and the road will be heading underneath the Docks, not over the top.

Soon enough we all heard of the grand plan of which this was just the slightest part. Each time I returned to the city there would be something new: the ring road working its way round from the north to the west to the south-west. Strange arterial roads sprouting to the south-east of the centre and apparently going nowhere. Then one night I took a wrong turn down one of these roads off a brand-new roundabout near the prison, and found myself heading down a deserted floodlit four-lane highway alongside a dockland inlet and there across the water, just off the eastern side of Butetown, is a giant pagoda, which on closer examination turns out to be the South Glamorgan County Hall.

At the time of writing, the visible signs of development are proliferating. To the east of Butetown there's the Atlantic Wharf development which consists of some refurbished warehouses, a new hotel, a reasonably tasteful housing development, and a big new waterfront fun-pub called The Wharf which has a mini shopping mall attached, as yet untenanted. To the south the Pier Head building has been refurbished and the waterfront is gradually being smartened up so you can now stroll for a fair distance either east or west from the Maritime Museum, and then visit the silly tube-like structure in which the plans for the development are displayed. To the east, over on the Grangetown side of the river, there's another big new housing development and the city dump has been cleared away in readiness for God knows what.

Turn back towards Butetown, cross James Street, where Lynette died, and pass St Clare's Court, where her friends Leanne Vilday and Angela Psaila lived, and you'll find yourself in Mount Stuart Square, the still-imposing heart of maritime, commercial, Victorian Cardiff. Now, though, the main industry based in Mount Stuart Square is the redevelopment industry. It's here, in Baltic House, that the Cardiff Bay Development Corporation has its HQ, and it's there that I went to talk to the CBDC's PR man, Derek Hooper, and to pick up an armful of their promotional literature, in an effort to make sense of the history and future of this redevelopment.

The beginnings were simple enough: the Docks had unarguably drifted into terminal decline and, in the mid-eighties, regenerating old docklands as business/leisure theme parks was all the rage from London to Baltimore. So, in 1985, South Glamorgan County Council decided to grab a piece of the action and went into partnership with Tarmac to redevelop the old Atlantic Wharf, to the east of Butetown; this redevelopment to be spearheaded by the building of the County Council's new headquarters at the southern end of the dock.

Next, the then Secretary of State for Wales, Nicholas Edwards, decided to get in on the act, and put forward a much grander plan which would cover the whole of the Cardiff waterfront, and would involve the building of a barrage across the Taff estuary, thus providing a brand new freshwater lake (and wiping out various strains of rare marsh-birds, but still, what's an omelette without a few broken gulls' eggs?).

Most everyone, give or take a few environmentalists and one or two of the people who actually lived in the docklands, thought this sounded like a mighty good idea. God knows, Cardiff needed some regeneration. So all that remained was to raise a couple of billion pounds and get on with the job.

Eight years after, it all started. The state of play is that around £450 million have already been spent, visibly so in the shape of assorted new roads, housing and business parks. And still most people think it's a good idea, even people in Butetown, though it's here that the arguments are fiercest. But the main debate is less about the rights and wrongs of the development as a whole and more about how much Butetown people will actually benefit from it.

The CBDC point to the new jobs, to the fact that a fair percentage of the new housing will be given to housing associations, to the community programme (new gear for the local sports teams, that kind of thing), to the jazz festivals and fireworks'n'fun extravaganzas they've been holding. Derek Hooper expresses their concern with maintaining the community's identity and generally puts the whole business forward as being for the best of all possible worlds, leaving me with an appealing tag line 'Butetown hasn't been a no-go area, people just haven't seen it as a place to go', and a manifesto: 'Cardiff can be one of the great maritime cities of the next century. That's our objective. And we want Butetown to participate in that as much as possible.'

The more cynical locals complain that the festivals and the community programme are little more than window dressing, that the new jobs are going to people from out of the area, that, as far as the new housing goes, they are much more likely to be offered a place on a dumper estate like St Mellons than in one of the shiny new waterfront developments. Such cynics suspect that the real plan is for the indigenous population to be moved out and the mythical yuppies to be moved in. And if they lack hard evidence for such a viewpoint, they can still point at the CBDC's promotional literature and its idealized portraits of the future docklands – portraits in which black people are conspicuous only by their absence.

As yet, though, the case has to be proven one way or the other. It's the next stage of the development that may well have the greatest effect on Butetown. Up till now most of the works have been carried out around the fringes of the peninsula, but the Bute Avenue scheme, planned to begin in 1993–4, will change all that. The railway embankment running parallel to Bute Street has traditionally been the community's eastern boundary and bulwark. The plan is for the embankment and railway line to be removed and replaced by a broad avenue, with a tram-carrying central reservation, sweeping north from the Pierhead to a new square near the Custom House, then forging a new wider link to the Monument and the centre of town.

Now the implications of this change for Butetown are hard to imagine. To be no longer an island below a bridge, but a residential neighbourhood within the heart of a shiny new maritime city, will surely strike deep at the community's identity.

One thing, however, is for sure: any project that's counting on raising £2 billion worth of private investment cannot have been too thrilled by an event like the killing of Lynette White happening on its doorstep.

THREE

Butetown Days, Part One

For me, it started on August Bank Holiday Monday, 1991. Taking the train down to Cardiff from London Paddington, heading for the Butetown Carnival. The weather was set fair, the train pleasingly empty, all in all a disconcertingly pleasant way to start an investigation into a murder.

Of course that wasn't really the start. The actual beginning was maybe three years before when I read the newspaper reports of the murder; or three months before when this book was first mooted; or when I started reading all the clippings and calling up the defence solicitors; or maybe even the week before when Tony Paris's solicitor had sent me along to see his cousin, Hughie Smith, and he'd suggested I come back for the Carnival, to be sure to meet all the defence campaign folks.

But this journey still felt like a start. Up to this point I'd been blundering about in the dark, trying to envisage the reality behind the headlines. And if late August sunshine did not seem appropriate to walking those mean streets, it at least provoked a sense of optimism in me as I arrived at Cardiff Central station, two hours out of London.

The Butetown Carnival has been running for more than a decade, but it's ten years since I lived in the city, and I wasn't even sure where it was being held these days. Still, Butetown's a small enough place so I figured I would find out. I turned right out of the station, past the monument, and right again to head under the railway line and into East Canal Wharf, where there's now no canal but a smattering of light industry and a car park used by the Custom House prostitutes to accommodate their less demanding punters.

No hustlers on parade today, though, just a stream of people walking in the same direction as me, heading towards the increasingly audible sounds of the carnival. I cut across the arterial road, Tresillian Way, and carry on past the old mosque and some more light industry (including a firm called Wyndham Engineering which, a couple of years ago, took over the business that had been in my family for the four generations prior to mine, John Williams Steel) before emerging into open space, the Butetown park that runs alongside Butetown's housing.

In front of me, but facing in the opposite direction, is the stage. As I get closer the music becomes identifiable as African, more or less. In front of the stage, spread out on the grass, are several thousand people. As I make my way through them, they're revealed as a remarkably mixed bunch, hippies and straights, black and white, young and old. People are drinking cans of lager or Coke, rolling spliffs or sleeping in the sun. Around the periphery of the crowd are a range of stalls offering hot dogs or pictures of Haile Selassie, Clark's pies or curried goat. Relaxed applause greets the end of the African combo's set and turning back to look at the stage I notice, waving above it, a giant banner proclaiming the support of the Cardiff Bay Development Corporation.

It's four o'clock, time to meet Hugh Smith. I head out of the park, past the ring of stalls and into residential Butetown. There's a sound system set up in my path, winding up the volume and attracting the attention of some of the youth. On my right the estate pub, the Paddle Steamer, is doing a brisk trade in takeaway cans of Red Stripe. Ahead are the Loudoun Square flats, the fourteen-storey tower block where Smith lives.

As council-run tower blocks go, however, Loudoun Square is a livable enough place; the lift works, doesn't smell of urine, and my fellow passengers look neither menacing nor terrified. Get out on the third floor, walk down the corridor and Hughie Smith turns out to be nowhere about. No surprise here, on a day like this it's easy enough to forget your appointments.

Back out in the park I set about trying to find Hughie

in the crowd, when I notice a small stall sporting a poster advertising the claims of various individuals to be wrongly imprisoned, plus a notice inviting me to sign a petition in support of the Butetown Three. I walk over and sign the petition and ask the blonde woman in charge of the stall if she's seen Hugh Smith. Yes, she says, hang on a minute, and runs off into the crowd shouting 'Hughie!'

Moments later she returns with Hughie, a personable shaven-headed chap in a track suit, plus another guy, light-skinned and wiry. Hugh proceeds to explain that this is Malik Abdullahi, brother of the imprisoned Yusef, that the blonde woman is Malik's wife, Alex, and that between them they are effectively running the defence campaign. I introduce myself and Malik starts to give me the third degree, trying to find out what my line is, whether I've already made up my mind as to the guilt of the Butetown Three. He's somewhat wary on this account following a recent feature in the *Guardian* which relied on considerable help from the defence campaign but ended up uncritically accepting the police's version of the case.

Still, it's too pleasant a day and Alex and Malik are too new to the business of dealing with the media to keep up the hard-nosed approach for long. Soon enough I've managed to reassure them that my mind is far from made up, and we've arranged that I'll come round to their house next week to talk some more and have a look at the defence campaign's hoard of documentation on the case. Meanwhile back to the carnival.

The festivities gain pace and pass in a blur of Red Stripes, herbal cigarettes, old friends bumped into, Cardiff's very own black rock combo (the imaginatively named Black Rocky Band) playing ZZ Top and Bob Marley covers, Shabba Ranks on the sound systems and, at nightfall, an adjournment to the White Hart, the pub now managed by Pete McCarthy, land-lord of the Custom House in Lynette's day.

Sitting in the pub and ruminating on the day, the real peace-fulness of the occasion is striking. In considerable contrast to the Notting Hill Carnivals of recent years, I saw only two police officers during the whole afternoon, and the overall atmosphere was startlingly reminiscent of the best side of the seventies.

The following week I've driven down to Cardiff and I'm steering the car down Bute Street, looking for Alice Street. I turn right into Hannah Street, a fifty-yard stretch featuring a church no bigger than a garden shed on the left, and on the right at the end the new Butetown Mosque, a sixties red-brick effort. Turn left at the mosque and I'm in Alice Street, a hundred yards of sixties council-built terrace housing. Alex and Malik's place is swiftly identifiable from the poster in the window.

Knock on the door and a young woman I haven't seen before answers, finds out who I am and ushers me away from a front room apparently full of children up to a first-floor sitting room. Malik will be down in a minute, she says. Would I like a cup of tea? Soon enough Malik does appear: he bursts into the room, radiating a near-dangerous level of energy and talking at least nineteen to the dozen – great developments are afoot, a man has walked into a police station in Dublin to confess to the murder! Had I heard? Did I know there had been a spontaneous march led by mothers and children from the local school in response to this news? Anyway what could he do for me? Would I like to see the papers – look around you, all these boxes are full of papers and that's hardly a fragment of the total. You should see how much stuff Rosie Paris has! OK, look at that box. Now let me play you this . . .

And Malik pauses for a moment as he plays me a song recorded by a group of local musicians to help the cause. I'm fearing the worst – an agitprop rant called 'Free the Butetown Three' – but instead I'm confronted by a stark and melancholic lament, an acoustic Butetown blues proclaiming that 'they done put the wrong man away'. And, for a moment, on Malik's face there's a trace of the pain of having his brother in jail for life for a crime which he believes him to be innocent of.

And then the doorbell rings, a woman calls 'Mal, it's for

you' and he's bubbling again. 'Stay here, have a look at the papers, I'll be back.' Malik reappears momentarily to introduce me to the visitor, a short guy with long dreadlocks who turns out to be Lloyd Paris, Tony's brother, before they disappear further upstairs.

So I'm left alone with the evidence, box upon box upon box of statements made to the police. I empty out a couple of boxes and start to sort through them: ten consecutive statements from Ronnie Actie, one of the original five accused, each running to eighty or so pages, reams of unused witness statements taken from practically anyone who has ever lived in the Docks or driven a car past the Custom House, and so on.

The unused statements have a particular fascination. The statements from the five accused tend to run to page after page of denials and circular discussions of alibis, but this unused material – semi-random intrusions into people's lives – has a hypnotic quality. It's stranger than fiction in the way that a fly on the wall documentary like 'Sylvania Waters' is always going to be weirder than any soap opera. On this preliminary trawl, for instance, I am suddenly drawn into the awful life of a young Asian woman who shared a flat with one of Lynette's prostitute associates. This illiterate young woman had been thrown out by her family and found herself, courtesy of cruel fate, thrust into the company of a group of lesbian prostitutes, expected to relinquish her bed if her flatmate brought a woman home for the night. She told the police that she couldn't manage the rent and her options seemed to have boiled down to either committing suicide or becoming a prostitute herself. Oh, and she knew nothing about either Lynette White or her murder.

An hour or so of wading through this kind of off-hand history of contemporary alienation and Malik reappears. He starts talking about himself a little. He's twenty-six, he's been in prison more than once, most lately in Dartmoor. He has been a family man for several years now. He has some seven children, four of them with Alex, ranging from a baby to a twelve-year-old. And is that easy to manage? Yes, he's says, the women all know each other, it's all right. And he tells me about how he and Alex finally got married last year; Malik won a sizeable amount on the horses and used it to fund a wedding party of such opulence that people have barely recovered from their hangovers a year or so later.

I ask him if he knew Lynette and he says 'Yeah, I used to get along with her well, she was all right. But she was a hustler, you know.' And then he says, as does almost everyone I'll meet in the Docks, 'If I knew who'd done it, no matter who they might be, I'd tell the police. If I believed it was my brother had done it, then he could rot in jail.'

We talk a little more and Malik agrees to help put me in touch with people involved in the case, but suggests that first I read some more of the statements to get a clearer picture of who I'll want to speak to. So I load up a couple of boxes of statements and head downstairs where I'm introduced to the kids: two girls, eleven and twelve, Gemma and Leanne; two boys, five and six, Malik and Rashid – Rashid after the third of the Dullah brothers, also currently experiencing Her Majesty's hospitality in Dartmoor.

Back in Alice Street, downstairs this time with Alex and the kids, sitting on the three-piece suite, facing the TV and video, behind us a breakfast bar, separating living area and kitchen. I'm waiting for Malik – something I'm going to get used to – on this occasion to be given the guided tour, Butetown by night.

Before little Malik can complete his attempt to dismantle me, Malik senior comes downstairs, and we're off. Out the back door, down the alley and we're on Bute Street. Turn to our left and we're outside John Actie's house. And, as luck would have it, John is just coming out of his front door, accompanied by his dog, General.

John Actie and General are pretty much living proof of the adage about dogs resembling their owners. John Actie is a light-skinned black guy with the build of the rugby forward he might have been, and a way of holding himself that bristles with barely contained aggression. His bearing suggests that he knows the world is out to get him and that all that he has to protect him is his physical strength. General is a Rottweiler whose evident aggression seems to be controlled only by his master's iron grip. Otherwise General looks eager to live up to his breed's reputation. It's clear that it takes most of John's strength to prevent General from converting us into a mid-evening snack. A tear in the sleeve of John's leather jacket testifies to the trickiness of his task, and the prospect of what might happen if man and dog were united in the charge of their aggression scarcely bears thinking about.

Still, I do my best not to give General the impression that I might be in any way terrified of him and John agrees to come over to Malik's later for a talk, once he's taken the dog for a walk. Meanwhile we head onward, up Bute Street towards town. We pass the Loudoun Square shops, open till late, and keep going till we arrive at the Custom House.

The Custom House is basically a bog-standard Cardiff pub, circa 1960. There's a Lounge bar that makes a feeble gesture at gentility but that's closed most of the time now and, anyway, the pub's focus has always been the Public bar. This is a room about fifty foot by fifteen, lino on the floor, a pool table in the middle, towards the front entrance a juke box, and a bar taking up half the length of the room, set in front of the back wall.

Tonight the clientele are occupying their usual positions. Older hustlers, the women it's barely credible can still be making a living at this game, are sat at the far end of the bar or at the couple of tables furthest from the front entrance. Scattered around the room are an assortment of men, either old and damaged or young and hard-eyed. Sitting round the pool table are a group of lesbians and younger hustlers. Playing pool as we enter are a dreadlocked lesbian and a drunken Irishman who is playing with the extravagant care of the truly pissed.

Malik doesn't want to stay in here; the case has caused too much bad blood. His brother, after all, used to work here and the working girls are wary. At best, he says, if they see me with him, they'll only tell me what they think Malik wants them to say. Better I should come back alone.

Out of the Custom House we head under the bridge to the fringe of the city centre, 'town'. Malik heads to our left and into a hotel that I remember as the Central Hotel, a place that has forever been clinging to a veneer of luxury and is now called the Diplomat. Through the lobby and Malik suggests that if I wasn't here they'd likely as not have refused him entry. Up the stairs and through a couple of doors and we're in a function suite currently being occupied by the Socialist Workers' Party. They're having a debate on racism and Malik has been invited to come along. We've missed most of it but catch the summing up and the questions after. Regular kind of affair, earnest students setting the world to rights. Malik gets the chair to announce an upcoming public meeting with Gerry Conlon from the Guildford Four as guest speaker. Mission accomplished we slip out and head back into Butetown.

This time we take the back way, East Wharf Road, the route Lynette White would walk each evening, taking the money to Miller. We pass the Bosun where Miller would be sitting in his car, and carry on down Angelina Street. Along the way Malik points out where the Free the Boys graffiti has been painted out, and then we arrive at Loudoun Square to call into the community's newest business, Cyril's Store. Cyril is a serious rastafarian who accompanies us to the Paddle Steamer, the currently very dead estate pub, and agrees to come by later and talk. As does his fellow member of Butetown rastafarian brotherhood, the Inited Idren, Keith Morell.

Pick up some Red Stripes from Cyril's and it's back to Malik's where Alex graciously includes me in their late-evening meal, a fine curry of Somali extraction, a dish Alex has learnt from her father-in-law via her mother-in-law, Pauline, Malik's white, Cardiff-born mother.

Another month later, a Saturday. I'm sitting upstairs and Malik is showing me photos of last week's excitement, the visit of Gerry Conlon from the Guildford Four, who'd come to speak at a public meeting and generally lend his support to the campaign.

While the support of Gerry Conlon might have little positive influence in the corridors of power, it has proved a tonic to the fledgling Cardiff campaign. Conlon had come down to Cardiff in the company of a prison buddy who had been released just a few days before, and the pair of them had shown precisely the kind of eagerness for a good time you might expect from people who'd spent a decade or so behind bars. So the campaign spared little effort or expense in providing them with a good selection of earthly comforts. Suffice to say that there's scarcely a picture of Gerry without a pint mug in his hand and that by the second day's snaps there's hardly a pair of eyes to be seen that are less than the deepest red. Everyone has let off a lot of accumulated steam and Gerry has become an honorary Docks boy, if such a thing can be.

A week later, though, the mood is somewhat hung over. Malik, in fact, has come down with a stomach bug and in subdued mood suggests I go with Lloyd to have a look at the murder flat, before we all head off in search of Ronnie Actie, a man who has, as yet, been having very little to do with the campaign.

Lloyd shows up, sporting a blue track suit with 'Free the Butetown Three' emblazoned on the back, and we get in his car to drive the hundred yards round to James Street. Park the car and Lloyd suddenly launches into a ferocious karate kick directed at a poster stuck on the wall. Turns out he has nothing in particular against Guns'n'Roses, or whoever, but does have a head full of terrible frustration that needs occasional physical expression. Then he explains the advantages of karate for a shortarse like himself, or indeed myself, before telling me that though Tony was the older boy it was always him who had to do the fighting for both of them. And here he is again: fighting for Tony.

Knock on the door of 7 James Street and down comes Carlton to open the door. Carlton, a middle-aged, somewhat grizzled guy with a marked West Indian accent, is Lloyd's and Tony's cousin, and he's now living in the murder flat – on the one hand ensuring access for the campaign and on the other hand providing somewhere for him to live, these being hard times for Carlton. As he ushers us up the stairs and right back along the corridor into the living room, he apologizes profusely for the state of the place, making it clear that this is not what he has been used to, nor what he wishes to become used to.

Sitting us down, he offers us some whitefish cooked West Indian style, and while he goes to the kitchen I'm able to look around the room. It's cosy enough now, with a Calor gas fire, sofa, chairs and TV, but the lick of paint can't hide the bloodstains on the walls. Still, it's been the commonplace for journalists to stress the bleakness, the squalor of this room, to emphasize the unutterable grimness of Lynette White's lonesome death, but, as Carlton says, returning with three plates of fish and two bottles of hot sauce, there is no apparent sense of evil here. He has spent months in this room but it has not oppressed him, and he believes that Lynette's soul, at least, is in peace.

Certainly it's easy enough to relax here, and soon the conversation moves on to Butetown in the old days. Carlton starts out by stressing to me that Butetown people have always made an honest living, working on the ships or whatever. The pimps and the prostitutes, he says, have always been outsiders, not the real Bay people. Lloyd however is more cynical, impatient too at the idea that there's much difference between honest work and dishonest in the Babylonian confinement of this society. 'It's all hustling,' he says, and Carlton is prepared to go along with that.

Now he's starting to relax and letting slip a little of his gentility. Soon Lloyd and Carlton are locked in a classic family argument, Carlton coming the knowledgeable old-timer as he argues the merits of street fighting against karate. And then it's time to move, thank Carlton for the fish, head back in the car to Malik's and onward in search of Ronnie Actie.

Ronnie's been holed up in his home turf of Gabalfa, an insular suburb tucked away between a couple of arterial roads towards the north of the city. First port of call is a pub called the Crown where Ronnie is rumoured to hang out playing pool with his spar, Johnny Crook. Malik dives in and receives the tip that we should try Ronnie's dad's house, down the hill, look for the place with all the cars outside.

Ron Actie senior is in, a big tall man who looks to have walked right out of the old photos of the bay: a working man out of a social realist propaganda poster. Malik and Ron step inside to chew the fat while Lloyd and myself wait in the car. Lloyd is feeling frustrated with the way the campaign is progressing. As he sees it, Malik and himself are doing all the work, keeping the flame alive, while John and particularly Ronnie Actie are just happy to be out, have forgotten their brothers back inside.

Malik returns with directions to Ronnie's current abode, just around the corner. We get there just in time to meet Ronnie on the doorstep, heading out for a Saturday-night meal with his wife. He looks less than thrilled to see us but says he'll call Malik tomorrow and sort something out for the afternoon.

So we head back over towards Butetown, stopping off for a Wimpy on the way. Malik's still not feeling too good, but decides to risk a pint anyway. We carry on to the Grangetown end of James Street and park by the Avondale, on the edge of Rat Island, the corner of the docks that survived sixties redevelopment unscathed. The Avondale is a singularly unprepossessing pub on the outside but its interior is pleas-antly reminiscent of a ship's cabin, an effect enhanced by the quantity of nautical memorabilia on the walls. Rat Island is a clannish community even by Butetown standards – so much so that Malik tells me that it took years of drinking here for Lloyd and himself to be accepted, despite the fact that they've spent most of their lives no more than four hundred yards away.

Inside the pub Lloyd moves about, talking to the people, while Malik and myself play a little pool. But once he's finished

47

his drink and lost a match, Malik decides enough is enough and heads back home to lie down and nurse his stomach. Come closing time, Lloyd and I decide to see a little more of the night life. First, however, Lloyd has a couple of things to attend to.

We head round to Lloyd's house, just along the way from Malik's. Into the living room and there's his wife, Sharon, lying asleep on the sofa in front of the TV curled up with their daughter, Shanice. Sharon mumbles a bleary hello and heads upstairs. Lloyd sits me down amidst his sports trophies, guitar and hi-fi in the front room, and follows her up.

Five minutes later we're on the move again, drive down Bute Street and then head west towards Splott, pull up in a car park behind a short terrace of houses. Wait here, says Lloyd. Fifteen minutes and he's back, mission evidently accomplished, and we're on our way back up Bute Street to the Big Windsor.

The Big Windsor is another remnant of the old bay. It's a pub-cum-boarding house that for years housed the city's first and best French restaurant. Now it has escaped the CBDC bulldozer but is still a shadow of its former self, closed much of the time, opening sporadically at weekends, when it will stay open late for dances. Last time I'd been there, to hear a reggae sound system, it had been almost empty.

Tonight, though, it's different. There's a vintage soul/r&b band playing, with a disco in the same vein, and the place is packed. Which isn't surprising: r&b has been the only kind of local live music to pull a crowd in Cardiff for as long as I can remember. The band is fine, if a little four-square rhythmically, and the mixed crowd are enjoying themselves, whether the dancing students at the front, or the smoke-wreathed locals standing around the edges. And soon enough things begin to blur. As the night draws on and mellows it is indeed possible to see the famed Butetown underworld operating. The Windsor is full of ganja smoke, cocaine and even rock cocaine is in evidence, as too are the wheelers and dealers – folk coming in and out of the club by the back door, that kind of scene.

And who knows, maybe some of the wheelers and dealers here tonight are big-time bad men who like to spend their days hanging out outside school playgrounds selling nose candy to the kids. But I doubt there's much of that; this feels like a small-time, small-town scene. Though there's evidently a demand for cocaine, particularly rock or crack cocaine – small wonder in a place with as little apparent future as Butetown – ganja seems, after all, the Butetown drug of choice, even ahead of alcohol.

And so, eventually, to bed.

FOUR

Lynette, Leanne and the Custom House Beat

The Monday before she died, 8 February 1988, Lynette White had a fight with Stephen Miller. She told him she knew he was seeing another woman; he told her she was a lying cow and as he puts it 'just gave her a slap – she started slagging me out and I gave her a slap'.

Before the row Lynette had been to work. Late afternoon Stephen had dropped her off on the corner of Bute Street and Crichton Street, just by the Custom House pub, the city's traditional prostitute hangout. Maybe she had a can of Breaker in the pub first, talked to the hustlers at the bar or the lesbians by the pool table. More likely to have been the latter. These were the women she hung out with, lesbian pimps like Debbie Paul, Maxine Campbell or Rita Pace, the one they call Rita Gas, thanks to her fondness for inhaling the stuff, and lesbian hookers like her best friend Leanne Vilday or Nicola Heysham. Maybe she had a spliff too, maybe even a little speed from her friend Leanne to help her through her shift on the beat. Because that's where she spent most of that evening, out on the Crichton Street beat waiting for the cars to stop, the windows to roll down, and the men inside to ask if she was doing business.

When it came to the business, Lynette was twenty and a veteran. She'd been on the beat since she left home at sixteen. Before that all the docks boys knew that she'd give it away. Jackie Harris tells a story about the time Lynette, aged fourteen or so, hostessed a gang bang in a tent in Bute park, and there is scarcely a man involved in the case who didn't have sex with her some time. She was a pretty blonde girl and she was a slag, a scrubber, a nympho, a good-time girl; and when she left school and home she knew she had one thing to sell, so she became a slag, a scrubber, a tart, a hustler, a lost girl.

It wasn't a pimp who put Lynette out on the beat. In Cardiff at least it scarcely ever is. That's putting the cart before the horse. Once a woman's on the beat, then her boyfriend or, likely as not, girlfriend will share in the profits and become a *de facto* pimp. But the TV image of the pimp, the guy with the hat, the cigar and the gun, has little connection with the tawdry reality of hustling outside the Custom House. From the summer of '86 on, though, Lynette managed to find herself the nearest approximation to a traditional pimp available.

Stephen Miller was nineteen when he came down to Cardiff from Brixton to meet up with his brothers, Tony and Mark, who were spending time there. Older brother Tony was living with Francine Cordle, a woman whose four brothers have achieved varying degrees of local celebrity in fields as diverse as Rugby Union and armed robbery. But Tony eventually went back to Brixton. Mark also returned to London and anyway had little part in the dealings of his brothers. 'He works and everything, right. He doesn't do nothing, you know what I mean,' his brother Stephen told the police when his name came up.

Stephen liked what he saw in Cardiff. He liked Francine's friend Lynette White and he liked the bad-man status he acquired by virtue of coming from the big city. He started spending more and more time in Butetown, and when Lynette asked him to live with her in her room in a house in Grangetown, he came to stay.

Two years later Miller had acquired a couple of mates, Eugene Savage and fellow London exile Pepsi Orton, a nickname 'Pineapple' – donated by Lynette's work mates in appreciation of the way he piled up his locks on his head – and a considerable cocaine habit. During the years Miller spent in Cardiff cocaine was the boom drug; unheard of quantities were making their way into the country, and no longer were supplies destined mainly for the middle-class recreational user. A significant new development had large quantities coming in via staging posts in the West Indies. A lot of coke was being funnelled in through Britain's black communities and some of it was staying there. Cocaine was starting to mimic its American odyssey from upscale recreation to underclass addiction. The price had dipped from anything up to £100 a gramme to around £60 a gramme. Stephen Miller's habit ran at around a gramme a day.

Snort up a line of coke and the world is a brighter sharper place, with you the brightest sharpest individual on its face; come down and there's a cloud of paranoid, violent depression waiting for you. Miller decided to keep bright and sharp all the time. And, seeing as how his girlfriend had a job, he felt that it was only fair that she should provide him with life's basic necessities, to the tune of anything up to £60 a day.

It's one of the stranger and sadder features of this story that Lynette White, nineteen and living in a rented room in Grangetown with two changes of clothes to her name, must have earned, in the last year of her life, somewhere between thirty and forty thousand pounds, tax free. It could have bought them out of their lives; instead it went up Stephen Miller's nose, into maintaining his sharp, bright, brittle front, the Brixton boy with attitude.

On an average day, Miller and White would drive the mile or so over to Butetown in the early evening. Lynette would stand out on the beat, often on her own, the first to arrive, and Miller would make his rounds. By eight o'clock he'd be parked outside the Bosun pub, be sitting in the car with a glass of brandy and a noseful of cocaine. Between eight and nine Lynette would call by with the evening's profits so far. Then it would be back to work for her, another drink for him and, after the pubs closed, a move up to the North Star where Lynette would show up as soon as she'd made enough money to keep Miller happy, sometimes as late as 1 a.m.

The North Star and the Custom House bookend Butetown.

The Custom House is at the northern tip and provides prostitutes for the good citizens who would be reluctant to venture any further into Butetown. The North Star is at the southern tip, close by the entrance to the actual Docks, and provided late-night drinking and relaxation for the working girls, plus, when the ships were in, a place for sailors to find themselves a hustler. The North Star was one of the principal places in which Lynette and Stephen played out their lives. It's a small enough building, a former Seamen's Mission, a chapel-sized place kept bible-black inside. On a typical night Miller would be standing at the back of the club with Eugene or Pepsi, and Lynette would be at the bar with her mates.

Lynette's mates here were the same bunch she hung out with in the Custom House, the group of lesbian hustlers and pimps. But while Lynette certainly knew a lot of people, it's difficult now to glean to what extent they were friends. For everyone who now describes her as a bubbly, happy-go-lucky girl who loved to be in the middle of the party, there's another to say she was a mouthy loner with a fondness for attention-seeking that made her a malicious gossip, a police informer and a woman notorious on the beat for trying to steal other people's clients.

Still, the group that Lynette was closest to was the loosely knit group of lesbians, and amongst them her two closest friends were a nineteen-year-old hustler, Leanne Vilday, and a mixed-race pimp, Debbie Paul, who was conducting an affair with Leanne at the time of the murder. And on this Monday night at the beginning of February, Lynette had little reason to be bubbly. She had heard that Miller was seeing another woman, Maria Veysey, and was winding herself up to have it out with him. Plus she was starting to worry about one of her upcoming court appearances.

Lynette's reputation for having a word in the law's ear was well deserved. She was due to appear as a witness in two criminal trials in the next few weeks. One case involved two men from Newport trying to put an under-age girl out on the streets. The other arose out of an incident in the North Star

Club. A prostitute, Tina Garton, had been stabbed in the lung, allegedly by Francine Cordle (who was eventually acquitted of this charge), and Lynette was to be a witness.

When she finally met up with Miller that night the anticipated row broke out. But by the end of the night they'd reached some kind of reconciliation. They left the North Star together and went back to their place in Dorset Street. According to Miller they went into the living room, watched a porno video and then had sex on the floor, before going up to bed.

Next day, and again according only to Miller, everything still seemed to be OK and, as usual, he dropped Lynette off on the beat in the late afternoon. Miller says he never saw her again. She didn't appear at the Bosun that night, and he waited in vain for her at the North Star.

There seems to be general agreement as to where Lynette went that night. Late in the evening she caught a cab, driven by Jack Ellis, the North Star Club's resident driver. She was clearly agitated and looking to find a place to spend the night away from home. The most popular explanations for her reluctance to go home are either that she didn't want to go to court to testify against Francine, or that she had failed to earn enough money for Miller and was terrified of his inevitable rage. Either way she tried various addresses around Cardiff without any luck. Finally she decided to head back to Butetown and try Leanne Vilday, who was currently staying with another prostitute, Angela Psaila, in St Clare's Court, a new block of flats on West Bute Street, a stone's throw from the North Star.

On arrival Lynette pressed the intercom button, and spoke to Angela who told her to come on up. When Leanne arrived back soon after, Lynette gave her some money to get four cans of Breaker from the North Star, explaining that she didn't dare go there herself for fear of seeing Miller. Several of the North Star regulars confirm at least that Leanne did come in for some cans and some put two and two together at the time, having heard Miller ask where Lynette had got to.

Next day is where things get hazy. Leanne and Angela claim

Lynette left the next morning after a late breakfast at Bab's, and that was the last time they saw her alive. Vilday thought Lynette was using the flat in James Street, of which she – Vilday – was the tenant, though it was normally used only as a place to take clients. Leanne had given Lynette a key some while before, and let her use it as her place of business. And this is the explanation accepted by the police; that Lynette was hiding out in this grim, unfurnished, uncurtained flat in James Street, until the fateful day that Miller learned of her whereabouts.

Certainly Miller was doing his best to find her. Tuesday night he went back to Dorset Street without her, putting her absence down to the aftermath of their row. Next day he spent at Pepsi's waiting to find Lynette that night. Come the night she still hadn't surfaced so he went to the North Star and quizzed the regulars for information. Soon enough he gleaned the club gossip that she could be over at Angela Psaila's. Tony Brace the doorman may have told him; more likely it was Debbie Paul, Leanne's girlfriend. Debbie anyway offered to take him over there to set his mind at rest.

He took her up on the offer and they barged into Psaila's flat, finding the residents in bed and no sight of Lynette. Psaila and Vilday say she wasn't there – local gossip at the time speculated that she was hiding in a cupboard. Either way, Miller didn't find her. Nor did he find her during the next three days. He told their landlord, Paul Coombs, and he went down to the Custom House looking for her, but without success. Miller kept up his routine: Pepsi's place in the day, North Star at night. His search was conducted with the special intensity of a man who had lost not just his girlfriend but his supply of cocaine. Word of his plight rapidly circulated around the community.

And that's where time stops. Up to this point everyone is in agreement – police, witnesses, the eventual accused – this was the way things were three or four days before Lynette died. It's what happened next that remains a mystery.

*   *   *

The thing about the Docks is that it has a bad reputation, an evil reputation. If you go down there you'll be robbed or drugged or pimped. Or killed. This reputation is way out of line; when it comes to robbing and killing the Docks is one of the safest places to be in the city. The drugs and the pimping, though, these provide the fire without which there'd be no smoke. Illegal drugs and commercial sex are available in the Docks. But, of course, no one is going to force them on you. You'll find them if you know where to look.

What the people who spread Butetown's bad reputation signally fail to understand is that a certain amount of sex'n'drugs'n'reggae represents a lifestyle that is actually attractive, that people freely chose to become a part of it, find it more like life than living on a librium-fuelled housing estate halfway between Cardiff and the back of beyond. And Lynette White was one such person.

Her childhood was a mess. She was born in Essex in 1967, the daughter of twenty-two-year-old Terry White and his girl-friend Peggy Stone. Essex was where Peggy's parents lived, and for the next three years the family shuttled between there and Clive Street in Grangetown, where Terry's parents lived. By 1970 the relationship was on the rocks and Terry found himself a place of his own in Portmanmoor Road, near Splott on the eastern edge of the Docks. Peggy came back for a while, but things failed to work out and she returned to Essex, taking her older daughter Dawn with her, and leaving Lynette with Terry, who moved in his sister, also called Lynette, to help out. Further assistance was provided by a neighbour, Mrs Cundy.

Terry was running a scrap-metal business from his back yard. But in 1971 he was arrested for receiving stolen metal, convicted and sentenced to two and a half years in prison. Lynette went back to live with her grandmother in Clive Street. Terry was let out after serving thirteen months in Cardiff and Swansea. On release he struck up a relationship with Carol Cundy, the daughter of the woman who had helped with looking after Lynette in Portmanmoor Road.

Three months later Terry found work in demolition in

Wrexham, a dour industrial town in North Wales, and moved there with Carol, leaving Lynette with her grandmother for the time being. After a few months Terry got a council house in Wrexham and Lynette joined them. They remained in Wrexham for a year, during which time Terry and Carol had a son, also called Terry, before making the somewhat familiar return to Clive Street.

Once again this was a less than entirely happy arrangement. Terry started rowing with his father, George, and moved with Carol to the house of a friend, Brian Driscoll, along with Driscoll's wife and four kids, but leaving Lynette behind.

In 1976, when she was nine, Lynette's life finally acquired some degree of locational stability. Terry was given the council house in Llanrumney that he still lives in and Lynette rejoined the family. Lynette had started school in Grangetown, but now she transferred to Greenway Junior in Rumney and remained there until she went on to Rumney High School. Terry recalls, 'She was of average intelligence in school and received a fairly normal upbringing, even though I served periods of imprisonment and was away from home.'

During this time Lynette began to ask about her natural mother, and eventually met her once or twice. When Lynette was thirteen Terry and Carol finally got married. At school she performed adequately, getting into a certain amount of trouble for talking too much. She also began her drift into what her father saw as unsavoury company. He discovered that she was regularly visiting the house of a school friend whose mother was allegedly a prostitute. Terry demonstrated his disapproval by going round there and smashing the house up with a spade. Another time Terry saw Lynette and the prostitute's daughter talking to two 'coloured' boys in a car. This time he responded by 'smacking' Lynette.

Then Lynette acquired her first serious boyfriend, a young black guy from Ely called Mark Harris. He used to visit Lynette at home and Terry recalls that he used to gamble on the machines a lot, but 'he seemed a reasonable boy to begin with and I cannot ever remember seeing her marked.'

Reasonable or not, Terry was aware of his paternal duty and he offered to 'see to' Harris. Lynette, however, told her father not to and, as he recalls, that 'she would only ever go with black boys. I asked her the reason why but she could not explain, saying that she just liked them better.' Which was a really strange thing to say. Not strange to say she liked black boys, not even surprising – after all, there was enough black blood in the White family already – nor was it strange to say she liked black boys better, again not even unusual, but to say that she would only ever go with black boys suggests some deeper need or trouble.

Anyway, the rows continued until Lynette moved out, got on her back and found herself a job. First off, she lived in Paget Street with Harris. Then, in 1986, she hitched up with one of her several local admirers, packed up with her boyfriend and moved into this older man's flat. She and her new man would go most nights to Stripes, a club in Charles Street, in the centre of town, that was then popular with some of the Docks people. Her man liked it because he felt it was sufficiently far away from his wife, who might not have been best pleased to find out about Lynette.

At this stage Lynette was maybe at her happiest, earning decent money as a new face on the Despenser Gardens beat, not working too hard, clubbing most nights, taking up with this boy then that one, while having a regular thing with this guy. Meanwhile she had come to some kind of truce with her father. He saw her out on the beat once and the inevitable row ensued. She stopped coming home to Llanrumney but when Terry was in the Docks after that they would meet for a drink in one of his regular haunts, the Packet, the Ship and Pilot or the Docks Non-Political.

But for Lynette the centre never held for long and in autumn 1986 her boyfriend left town. Soon after this abandonment started Lynette called up one of her irregular boyfriends, the Londoner Stephen Miller, and invited him to move in with her.

Stephen Miller was nowhere near being the start of

Lynette's troubles: her childhood had been hard and she was already a prostitute; Miller even loved her after a fashion, which was something she had little enough of in her life; but he certainly made matters worse. He speedily became used to the money Lynette was earning, acquired a taste for cocaine and encouraged her to work longer hours to let his habit develop. By the end of 1987 she was a fixture on the Custom House beat, having been moved on from the Despenser Gardens stroll by one of the police's periodic crackdowns. She would be the first girl out at lunchtime, and the last one left at night. When they saw her working on Christmas Day, the other hustlers all agreed that Miller was pushing way too hard.

It was a difficult relationship for outsiders to read as it was mostly conducted in private. Miller wouldn't frequent the Custom House while Lynette was working, preferring to sit in his car outside the Bosun. They wouldn't even be together when they met up at the North Star late in the evening. Lynette would sit talking to her friends while Miller stood at the bar or at the back talking to Eugene or Pepsi. One of the few people who saw them together was the North Star's resident taxi driver, Jack Ellis, who offered the police a nutshell account of their romance.

'They seemed a very happy couple at first, and it would be a regular occurrence at the time that I would take them both home from the North Star, and stop at the Taurus Steak Bar so that they could purchase a takeaway meal. As far as I know they only ever purchased steaks. I don't recall them ever purchasing chicken meals. On the odd occasion I didn't take them to the Taurus I would take them to the Red Onion Pizza and Burger Bar, so that Lynette could purchase her burgers which she enjoyed.

'Later, when Miller purchased his own vehicle, I would only take Lynette home on the rare occasions that Stephen wasn't ready to meet her or he'd tell her to go home and he'd see her later on. On those occasions Lynette never seemed to have any money and wouldn't ask me to take her for a steak at the Taurus or a burger at the Red Onion.

'In the last two months I found Lynette had changed and become very sloppy in her appearance. She always wore the same clothes, a pair of jeans and a grey leather jacket and trainers. She would ask me to take her to the Casablanca or the blues, looking for Stephen. Around Christmas time I took her from the North Star and picked Stephen up from the Casablanca. I dropped them off in Clare Road and saw Stephen punching and kicking her.

'It was around that time that Lynette start talking a great deal to me. She'd complain that Stephen had given her a good beating and that she had bruises everywhere, but I only saw a bruise on her face once. She became very depressed and upset and would tell me that if she didn't earn enough money he would beat her up. She started becoming frightened to go home if she hadn't earned enough, and once I dropped her off at her auntie's house in Channel View, Grangetown. On another occasion she came with me and Tony Brace to the Cabbies Club after the North Star had shut. We stayed there for about two hours talking – till 6 a.m., that is. I then dropped her off at Dorset Street but she told me the next day that she didn't go in. She appeared nervous, but knowing her and knowing that she was getting blocked up on coke I thought it might have been the effects of that. I think on the times when she didn't go home she would walk the street and ring him in the morning.

'Since Christmas she wasn't her normal self. Whereas before she would be lively, all she would be doing was drinking by herself waiting for Stephen to come in, click his fingers and off she'd run. If she was a bit high she'd want to talk and if I had enough time I'd listen to her. She would always sound unhappy.'

Maybe the only other person to see much of Lynette and Stephen together was Debbie Paul – a woman whose name came up time and again in the early days of the investigation. A lesbian pimp, not only was she a friend of Lynette and Stephen, she was also Leanne Vilday's lover and was herself briefly a suspect during the investigation. I met her on a mid-winter evening in the Red Dragon bar next to the Central Station – a desolate gay club with black-painted walls and blood in the urinals. In person Debbie turned out to be a stocky, powerful black woman, thirtyish, dressed in jeans and a sports top, sporting dreadlocks and a gap-toothed grin, and possessed of a cheery disposition. As did the fact that her most evident sympathy for anyone involved in the case was reserved for Leanne Vilday's little boy, Craig.

Debbie started off by talking about Lynette: 'She was a nice girl. She was quiet, though on the beat she might get a bit aerated with the punters and chops off, which is natural. She went quieter again when she was with Stephen. She used to talk to me, there's things she told me she wouldn't tell anybody else. It was only me who went down to see them both.'

What she saw of them, however, tended only to confirm the general view of their relationship. 'When you see her on the beat at half past four in the afternoon and she's still there at 10.30, well, that's a long time to be on the beat,' said Debbie. 'She couldn't move off there until she had actually got the money he wanted. If she couldn't make it, there'd be pressure. She'd shit herself. Sometimes she'd say to me, "Paul, I've only got so much, he'll fucking kill me." That unfortunate figure of speech is one that Debbie remembers coming from Stephen's mouth as well: 'He used to get a bit upset if she was a bit late with a punter. He would go, "Where the fuck is she, I'll chop her head off." I think that was just a figure of speech. Whether he did get really heavy . . . I only once saw a bruise on her. Maybe he hit her from the neck downwards, I don't know. There's other ways to hurt people . . .'

As for Miller himself, she said, 'I thought he was weird, he was quite deep like, he kept himself to himself, he didn't mix. I'd sit in his car and have a smoke of coke with him, like, and then he'd come in and there might be loads of people with us and he'd buy me a drink, he wouldn't buy no one else a drink. But he was brilliant to me, I was the only one who Lynette could hang around with, out of all the lesbians. According to Stephen, he didn't like the community, the lesbian community. He didn't like lesbians. I said that's a bit stupid, why do you like me then? He said, "Oh, maybe it's because you're black." Fair enough.

'Stephen was a pimp, he used to live off immoral earnings, like I did. He was only a pimp on Lynette, as far as I know. He could only just about handle her, let alone anyone else. He was so ugly. He was really an ugly man for a black guy. He smelled, he stinks. But from the time he could make someone lay on their back and make him £100 a night, put it in his pocket, he's a pimp.'

And if Miller wasn't a pimp in the sense of a guy running a string of girls, he was certainly a pimp rather than just a boyfriend according to Debbie. 'Most of the girls are working for themselves,' she said. 'And some of the girls are working for their man as well. Round here the way it works is that if you've got a man dealing with drugs, and you've got a prostitute and they connect, then half of his money's with her, and half of hers is with him, it's all mixed together. If you've got a relationship with a pimp you've got to have some sort of agreement – I give you some of my money and you give me some of your money; you're making off drugs, you've got to compromise. But I don't think Stephen ever compromised, he would just take all the time. He would never give. Lynette would come round with a ring and say, "Look what Stephen bought me," and she don't realize it was off her own fucking back. She's lying on her back making money for him to buy her things – she thought that was kosher.'

Like Jack Ellis, Debbie noticed changes in the last weeks of Lynette's life, but more in Stephen than Lynette. 'When he used to come down to the North Star he'd be wary of all the other black guys. He'd stand in the corner on his own, or by me and Lynette, maybe with me and Eugene having a smoke. And he didn't go anywhere else. But a few weeks before Lynette's murder he started going up town. He was dressing up, looking kosher, going to Stripes or wherever, then picking

Lynette up after the club finished there, and going up to the North Star. That was only the last two or three weeks.'

As for Lynette, Debbie said, 'I saw her about a week before she died. She was talking a bit about getting away from Stephen, she asked me if she could use my flat to get away for a while, and I said, "Not particularly, Lynette," because I didn't want the pressure of a lot of black guys coming to where I live. There were other people living all around and I didn't really need the hassle of him going up there and smashing the door down or whatever trying to get to her, so I said no. But from there I don't know where she went, she just disappeared.'

Still, her friendship with both parties landed her in the front line when Lynette disappeared and Stephen started looking for her. 'On the Tuesday or the Wednesday he asked me if I'd seen Lynette and I said no, I hadn't. I said, "Listen, Steve, if you don't believe me you can come to the flat and have a look." So that's what we done. I took him over, checked the cupboards and whatever. He still went on saying, "One of you women, one of you lesbians, you know exactly where she is." I didn't. He never approached me again. He thought one of the lesbians knew and he said he just wanted to talk to Lynette. But whether it would have been straight talk or physical talk we didn't know.'

And that was the last of Debbie's involvement in the messed-up lives of Stephen Miller and Lynette White. Next thing Debbie knew, Lynette was dead and her girlfriend, Leanne, was pitched into the heart of the matter. But while Debbie was unable to offer much in the way of new light on what happened to Lynette, she did provide an unusually clear picture of life in the small world of the lesbian/prostitution scene. Debbie knows how things work. She could fix your car for you and she can explain the way things go in the Custom House. They're the pivots of this world, the lesbian pimps, part of it, contained within it, in a way the men never are, but not its foot soldiers either, like the working girls.

*   *   *

'I was sort of trapped up in Rumney with all my friends from school,' Debbie says, remembering how she came to Butetown. 'I knew there was nothing there for me. I knew there was something different. I used to go to the city, football and that. I used to hang around the station with the city boys. Then I started going to the Cambrian, first lesbian I ever met was in there. I went, "Wow, a real lesbian!" and she put me on to the scene, like. That was all right, not a bad scene. I was fifteen. I left home and I just sort of mingled in, and that's how I got into the community in Butetown. I used to go to the Cambrian pub, the Golden Cross – that used to be full of lesbians – the Custom House, Barrels, I just caught Barrels, and then there was another gay club in the Oxford Arcade, Hunter's.'

Debbie's thirty now and she spends most of her time with her girlfriend in Newport. She's distancing herself from the Custom House scene, a scene anyway that is not what it was, not since Lynette died, not since the North Star closed down. 'Before Lynette died that community was bubbling,' says Debbie. 'Since Lynette died that community has gone downhill. It's not so much the police closing places down – the main reason why places have closed down in the Docks is because they're making the fucking bay look bigger, y'know what I mean. Roads through this one, roads through that one.

'The North Star should have been knocked down years ago. There were rats roaming through there, they had nothing on pump, the beer was always in cans, cans of Breaker, cans of Black Label, cans of Heineken, the shorts were watered down but you still paid for them because the club stayed open to four, five o'clock in the morning. And we had a *good* time. If there was a big fight everyone would join in, and everyone would finish. If one of the ship guys wanted to cause shit with one woman he had to take on the rest of them. He wouldn't just get one kicking, he had have a kicking off the lesbians and another kicking off the fucking prostitutes.

'It was the type of club that if you came there they'd make you welcome. There were prostitutes, lesbians, queers, ship guys. If you didn't like the atmosphere, fuck off. Didn't charge the women to go in, charged the men a pound. Supposed to be a seamen's club. When Lynette was alive that club was jammed seven nights a week, after Lynette died that club wasn't packed at all. Before people would come down from the Valleys just to go to the North Star, because everyone used to have a good time.'

Prostitutes, lesbians, queers, ship guys . . . The lesbian scene in Cardiff, the world that Debbie Paul is part of, is not any kind of separatist scene, still less a feminist scene. This is not part of the 'political' lesbianism of *Spare Rib* or the *Guardian* Women's Page but out of an older, less visible, tradition, that of the lesbian as sexual and social outlaw. 'Well, prostitution here, it's a lesbian scene,' said Debbie. 'The majority of the prostitutes are lesbians, they're either lesbians or bisexual before they go on the game. That's why Lynette was hanging around with the lesbians. Lesbians, prostitutes and black men. That's how it is.'

Debbie Paul's other vital connection with the case was through her girlfriend Leanne Vilday, Lynette White's best friend and a central witness in this case. It was in her flat that Lynette was murdered and it was she who discovered the body. She was also the only major witness for the prosecution who even approached coherence in her testimony. She also seems to know more than anyone else, bar the actual killer, about Lynette White's last days.

Unfortunately, if unsurprisingly, she doesn't want to talk about it now. Even before the trial she wrote to a friend to say that the only way the police were going to leave her alone was if she testified that the five guys were guilty. So maybe she doesn't want to talk about it, she's certainly frightened too. 'Panorama' wined and dined her repeatedly in an effort to get her to come clean for the camera, and Malik felt that she was within an ace of doing so, but in the end they had to settle for some terrifying footage of Leanne relaxing with friends, including Maxine Campbell, at someone's flat.

Leanne is sporting a black eye picked up a day or two earlier when she'd had a row on the beat and someone had swung a plank into her face. Everyone's drinking Super Tennents in this overlit kitchen and the situation looks like it might be desperate if only anyone cared enough to make it so.

So Leanne wouldn't talk because she was caught between the devil and the deep blue sea. If she confessed that she had been lying, the boys might be set free, but who knows how they'd feel about her earlier role, and the police would be down on her like several hundredweight of bricks. Which is the last thing you need if you're doing Leanne's job. Which is the same as ever, only now her regular beat is over in Riverside.

Leanne is originally from Barry, a staggeringly ugly and boring town that used to be a giant coal and steel port, and is now a banana port and a toxic seaside resort. Best thing about Barry was always the Barry Island funfair. I used to go there as a kid, but they kept closing the rides down. Fun while it lasted.

Leanne Vilday is kind of typical: a girl who can scarcely be bothered to exist, someone who became a prostitute not out of desperation or by conforming to any fashionable theory of deprivation but because it was a really bloody easy way to make money. Five minutes in a parked car for the same money as eight hours behind a chip shop counter and less grease on your clothes at the end of the day. Get up in the afternoon, go to the pub, have a few drinks, a smoke, dab of speed and pop out for the odd half hour, drink some more, more drugs, go down the club. It's easy. That's why she did it. And of course it's horrible, but, unlike most horrible jobs, the hours are short and the pay relatively good and if it's dangerous, so's going down a mine . . .

To get much more of a picture of Leanne we'll have to rely on her statements to the police and on the testimony of her lover at the time of the murder, Debbie Paul, who recalls the beginnings of their romance:

'When I first saw Leanne,' recalled Debbie Paul, 'she was

with a girl called Rita Pace. I think Leanne started on the beat through Rita, 'cause Rita used to go out there, and Leanne used to go there with her, thought it must be easy money, like. I would just say hello to Leanne, then one time I said, "I'm going to have you one day," and years went by, like, and she wanted to get out of this relationship. So I said get your gear together and I packed all her stuff in my car and moved her over to Maria Jacobson's house. She was staying over there for a while and I started seeing her, sort of thing.

'Leanne, she's a very generous girl. Bit of a fucking Tom Pepper, she likes to lie for the sake of lying. I say, "Oh, you been to see so and so?" She says, "No, I stayed here," knowing damn well I knows that she's been there. I don't know with Leanne. She was shy until she got on the scene herself, and then the shyness sort of come away from her. She started opening up more.'

From Maria Jacobson's Leanne and Debbie moved to the new St Clare's Court block, into a flat belonging to a friend of Leanne's from the beat, Angela Psaila. And by this time Leanne had her baby Craig, whose father is Tony Paris's brother Paulie. Ronnie Actie reckons Angela helped out with looking after the baby, but Debbie disagrees: 'Angela wasn't looking after the baby, she wasn't capable of looking after a baby. She can't even look after her own baby, let alone look after my boy. I was looking after Craig, when Leanne was on the beat I'd be looking after him. Everywhere I went Craig would be with me.'

It was while they were living at Angela's that everything went to hell. Debbie remembers the first time she saw Leanne after the discovery of Lynette's body: 'Leanne opened the door and she went, "Oh, Paul." I said, "What?" She said, "They found Lynette," and she started crying for a while, not long, and that was the only time she cried, as far as I know. I just picked Craig up and started doing things around the house, I said, "I fucking told you she was over there." I said to her in the week, I said, "Fucking check your flat, she's probably over there." And she went, "Oh, I don't think so." After that she didn't show any feeling, she never even bothered with her fucking son. I think it was the pressure of the police and everything.'

Soon Debbie and Leanne's relationship began to fall apart, first there was a row with Angela, which resulted in Leanne moving out; then there were the drugs Leanne started injecting; and then there was her relationship with Ronnie Actie, which was the final straw for Debbie.

But what really pulled Leanne's life apart was Lynette's death. Debbie said, 'She changed after Lynette died. That girl couldn't be bothered to do anything. Her son, he was calling my mother "Nan". She turned into a dirty prostitute. There's clean prostitutes and there's dirty prostitutes. A clean prostitute uses a Durex and whatever, cleans herself up afterwards. Leanne used to come home and, instead of going to the bathroom, just get into bed. I'd say what the fucking hell's that smell, get out, get in the bath. You know, you could literally smell she'd come back from a punter, come back from whoever. I'd say get out of my fucking bed. You could smell the dirtiness on her. I couldn't handle things like that. It just made me sick. And there wasn't just me and her in the bedroom, there was Craig as well. He was in his cot, all this wafting about into his lungs.

'She didn't give a fuck. It had come to the stage that she didn't care a fuck about herself. She didn't care how she looked. She's one of those people if you slap her she'd have a bruise, and she's a bleeder, you just give her a little dig she'd bleed and that's how she'd leave it. Instead of washing her face and tidying herself up, she'd leave that blood all over herself. Her hands and nails were always dirty. If I didn't nag her to get in the bath she'd never get in the bath. The drugs shouldn't make no difference, I knows plenty of peoples who jack up and they still gets in the fucking bath.'

And when Debbie broke up with her that was just the last straw: 'I think when Leanne found out I didn't care, she used to just shag anybody. I think Leanne shagged the whole of the fucking people [involved in the case]. Leanne got caught in bed with Tucker by his girlfriend. Fuck knows what she's got, she didn't care, she's sick. She makes me sick – the things people would come back and tell me she'd said, like I never gave her a kiss. Whoooo!'

Now Debbie feels mostly bitterness for Leanne, sees her as a self-made victim: 'One time I felt sorry for her – now I don't at all, I think she caused all this her fucking self. She should have thought about the people she hangs around with first.'

Lynette's death diverted the course of Leanne Vilday's life. The months that followed were spent talking endlessly to the police, as her hold on the basics of life slipped. And yet these statements provided less and less in the way of useful information; even a visit to a police-approved hypnotist yielded nothing new. What emerged instead, though, was a startlingly matter-of-fact account of the daily grind of a Custom House prostitute. Here, for example, is a day-by-day diary of Leanne Vilday's life in the week running from Monday 8 February to Sunday 14 February 1988, the day on which what little shape her life had acquired was to be shattered.

MONDAY: *I got the baby ready for bed. I like to see the baby settled before I go out to work. I went out between about 7 and 8 p.m. I went to the Custom House to do business. As far as I can remember I did about five or six punters and earned about £80. I finished my business and I joined my friends Debbie and Sarah for a drink. By the time we left the pub it was about twenty past twelve and I went to get a taxi but I ended up flagging a punter down. I asked him to give us a lift down to the North Star. He dropped Debbie and Sarah outside the North Star and I asked him if he wanted business. He said he did and drove his car into the car park opposite the North Star where I had straight sex with him; he paid me £10.*

When I joined Debbie and Sarah inside I had a few to drink. About three o'clock in the morning Ronnie Actie walked in. Ronnie Actie is my bit on the side. Debbie didn't know about Ronnie. Ronnie caught my hand and pulled me out of the North Star. He wouldn't take no for an answer so I got into his car and he took me to his sister's place in a big block of flats in Gabalfa. I slept straight through till 4 p.m., Tuesday.

TUESDAY: *When I got into the flat Debbie was there. She wanted to know where I'd been and all that. She told me if I went with Ronnie again she would finish the relationship. I didn't want to argue so I got ready to go out on my beat. I had about two or three punters. I went home about 11.30 p.m. and Debbie, Sarah and Angela were at the flat. I watched telly or listened to some music and went to bed.*

WEDNESDAY: *I got up when the baby woke up, about 10 or 11 a.m. I stayed in all day with Angela, Sarah and the baby. At about 8 or 9 p.m. after the baby was settled in bed and asleep I went out on my beat outside the Custom House. I didn't do very well, I had maybe two or three punters and I packed up about eleven and went home. About 2 a.m. I was awoken by Stephen Miller and Debbie Paul. Miller said he was looking for Lynette. I told him she wasn't in the flat but he could look around if he wanted to. He didn't bother and left.*

THURSDAY: *About 1 p.m. I went up to town. I walked up, with the baby in a pushchair. I did some shopping in the St David's Centre for baby stuff, like food and nappies. I went into Astey's Café for a cup of tea and returned home at around 5 p.m. I stayed in with Angela and watched the telly.*

FRIDAY: *Stayed in all day with the baby. About 8 p.m. I went down to the Custom House with Debbie. We had a drink together and about 9.30 I was approached by a punter called Paul from the valleys. He took me in his car down to St Clare's Court. After we had done the business the punter took me back to the Custom House. I stood outside for about five minutes and two blokes walked past. I asked them if they wanted business. One of them said yes so I did business behind Aspro Travel Agents. After we had finished he went one way and I went back inside the Custom House. The other bloke that had been with him asked for business and I took him to the same place. When I'd finished the punter left me. I had £40 now and I went back to the Custom House. Debbie and I decided to go to*

Barry on the train. In Barry we went to the Pixie Club and stayed there till it closed. We got a taxi back to St Clare's Court.

SATURDAY: *Saw to the baby. After putting the baby to bed I went out on my beat. First pick-up was four Pakistanis in a car. Three wanted to do business, one didn't. I got into the car with them to St Clare's Court. All of us went into the living room. Two of them followed me into the bedroom, one stood by the bedroom door and I did business with the other. The other two went down the shop while I was doing business with the second one. In the middle of doing business with the second one the bedroom door burst open. It was Maria Britto, Paulie Paris's missus, she wanted to see me about the baby. I told her to get out of the room and I got dressed. I told Maria to go in the bathroom . . . an argument ensued . . . Maria then hit me with her umbrella about the face causing two black eyes and a swollen nose. Maria left. I told the Pakis to go, I wasn't doing any more business. They left but about ten minutes later two of them came back. One of them did business with Angela. I cleaned myself up a bit. I got the baby out of bed and Angela, the baby and I picked up a taxi and went into town to the Red Onion. Angela ran in to get the burgers. I put the baby back to bed, got changed and put make-up on and went to the North Star getting there about twenty past three. In the club I met up with Ronnie Actie. We went to his sister's in Angelina Street.*

SUNDAY: *Rita Pace called at the flat between 9.30 and 10 a.m. to see the baby but as he wasn't awake I made her wait till he woke at about 11 a.m. We decided to go to Splott market and at 1 p.m. Rita went to Bab's Bistro to order a taxi but it didn't turn up. We watched 'Eastenders' till 3 p.m. Then Rita, the baby and I went out and picked up a taxi. We got to Splott Market about 3.15 and left there about 4 p.m. From there we went to Astey's Café and stayed there until about 5.30 p.m. because Rita was out. We got a taxi back and I got the baby ready for bed and myself ready to go out. Angela's boyfriend Teddy Ali called. We gave him money to do a taxi fare for us. So he took me, Rita, Angela and the baby to Broadway to buy gas for Rita. On the way back Teddy dropped me and Rita outside the Custom House and then took Angela and the baby home.*

Whatever grim routine Leanne had followed that week, the murder of Lynette White tore it apart.

FIVE

The Framing of Tiger Bay: Anatomy of a Fit-up

This is the way they found Lynette White. She was lying on her back in the front room of number 7 James Street, first-floor flat. Her right arm was outstretched, her left arm was bent upwards and was still in the sleeve of her black leather jacket. The rest of the jacket was wrapped around her chest. Her head was turned to the left, and most of her throat was missing.

She had two t-shirts on, a grey one over a black one. They were cut and cut and cut until they were lace-like and set stiff and brittle, soaked through with blood that was mostly dry by the time they found her. Below she wore stonewashed jeans that were cut on the inner left thigh. There wasn't much blood under her body but there was a large pool of the stuff a few feet away, nearer the bed, the room's only item of furniture. There was blood smeared and splashed on the wall, even blood on the walls of the passageway. She was fully clothed when they found her, apart from the half-off jacket and her right shoe which was lying near her left arm.

This is how Lynette White died. The man who killed her had a knife with a blade about an inch thick and at least five inches long. She fought him at first, took her first wounds on her hands and arms. He slashed her on the side of her left forearm, then stabbed the back of her arm. The next one she took on the thumb. He cut the back of her right hand and she stopped two more stabs with her ring finger and little finger. She bruised her right hand too, trying to fight him.

But he won. His next blow, too literally, was the killer. A full-blooded right-to-left slash to the throat. The blade went in below Lynette's right ear and cut diagonally downwards across the front of her neck, ending only at the angle of the jaw on the left side. Then he cut her throat again, starting lower on the right side of her neck but ending at the same point. It was as if he'd wanted to cut out her neck, as if he'd been trying to decapitate her by removing her neck. This wound opened her body, like taking the lid off a bottle. You could see muscles, tissue and the bones of her spine through it. Her larynx was cut in two at the point of the epiglottis. The right carotid artery and all the veins were severed as was the jugular on the left side.

She was dead now of course, but that wasn't the end of it for him, it was barely the start. Two score more stabs and slices before he was through.

He moved down to her chest now. He pierced her heart seven times in the frenzy that followed, pierced her lungs, her diaphragm, her liver. But it wasn't her heart or any vital organ he was aiming for. He was trying to cut her breasts off. No, maybe not to cut them off, but to obliterate them. Or why else was there a gaping stab wound between the upper part of her breasts, and another gaping wound in the upper part of her left breast? Why else did he stab the inner side of her left breast then stab and slash a huge gash lower down on the left breast and follow that with another slash that extended the wound all the way to the nipple, and stab twice more just below the nipple? And what he did to the right breast was worse, four gaping wounds followed by five stabs, two of which cut the nipple itself. And then six more stab wounds between the breasts.

This man destroyed her breasts. What he did was so terrible that the internal damage to her chest was such that the pathologist's report simply says, 'It is impossible to give a verbal description of this damage, but photographs were taken.'

He still wasn't finished. He kept moving downwards. Two stab wounds to the stomach were followed by a terrible slash to the belly. You could see a pad of fat poking out through the hole.

And then he stopped. Though he cut her face too, maybe earlier as they fought, cut her twice across the left eye. And there were other cuts to her chest and arms, and scratches that could not accurately be counted given the mess he'd made of her, but there were in all fifty wounds that were counted and numbered and filed away.

There were things he didn't do too, this man who butchered Lynette. He didn't rape her. Didn't take her trousers or her red panties off, didn't touch her genitals. If anything he seems to have killed her before she could get her jeans off. When she'd got out the condom and taken her right shoe off, just prior to taking her jeans off, that's when he seems to have snapped, to have killed her as quickly as he could, to have used all his force to chop out her throat and make her stop. And then punished her by annihilating her breasts, by chopping her belly. By de-mothering her.

This is what Lynette White left behind: the clothes she was killed in, three pairs of trousers, four skirts, three jumpers, four shirts or blouses, one sleeveless denim jacket, one anorak, one pair of tights, one pair of overalls, one suspender belt, thirteen pairs of knickers, two pairs of shoes, one pair of boots, a lock of Stephen Miller's hair.

First came the forensics. Fingerprints were found all over the flat. A bloody handprint was found on the wall, and some alien blood was found on Lynette's jeans. Furthermore the blood was from a very rare blood group, a potentially invaluable aid once a likely suspect was apprehended.

Meanwhile, the police started interviewing people: friends, relations, neighbours, potential witnesses. They started with those closest to Lynette. The closest person of all and, of course, the most obvious suspect was her boyfriend and pimp, Stephen Miller. He was interviewed repeatedly over the next few days, but to little effect. He said he hadn't seen her for days, and had no idea who might have killed her. And, as far as his credentials as a suspect went, he seemed genuinely upset, not to mention the fact that neither his fingerprints nor his blood type matched the forensic evidence found in the murder flat.

Next in line was Leanne Vilday. She was Lynette's best friend and it was her flat that Lynette's body had been found in. But she too claimed not to have seen Lynette for days and was ruled out of any direct involvement by the lack of forensic evidence.

Lynette's family were the other obvious interviewees but they knew little of her daily life, so that too proved a blind alley.

And so the police were forced to widen the net. Butetown speedily became a hot-bed of rumour and for the next few weeks the police were kept busy chasing up suggestions mostly made out of malice or ignorance. One early suspect was Peggy Farrugia, the Maltese mother of Francine Cordle. Peggy was thrown into the frame because of the Docks-wide fame of her terrible temper, combined with the fact that her daughter was due to appear in court on a serious charge to which Lynette was a principal witness. Peggy had put up enough backs over the years to be a popular choice for the role of killer, despite the fact that having a hot temper is hardly the same thing as cold-bloodedly murdering a witness. Anyway, the forensics exonerated her.

Other names given serious consideration at one time or another included the lesbian pimp, Debbie Paul, the gay man who lived upstairs, Mark Grommek, and even Malik Abdullahi, who wryly observed that the police were hardly being met by the clichéd 'wall of silence'. Instead half of Butetown was busily engaged in getting a word in edgeways.

Eventually they seemed to have got somewhere. A schoolgirl called Melanie Mail reported having seen a man with blood on his hands, sitting near the murder flat on the Sunday morning. Other sightings of this man were also reported. The police felt confident enough about these leads to take the story on to 'Crimewatch' in May. Chief of South Wales CID, John Williams, appeared on the show, presented a photofit of a white man with lank dark hair and exhorted the public to try to identify him.

But nothing happened. The man was not identified and the police were left with nothing else to do but carry on with the long-winded business of interviewing every prostitute they could find, and taking down the vehicle registration numbers of as many prostitutes' clients as they could, and then interviewing them.

The criminal investigation mounted in search of Lynette's killer was on such a large scale it became far more than an investigation into a single murder. It was the systematic laying bare of a community. It was a lifting up of stones on a grand scale, and what was revealed was too often misery. Take, for instance, the volumes of statements taken by the police from men identified as kerb crawlers or punters. Meditate for a moment on the bleakness in the statement taken from Martin Thomas (for legal reasons, the names and identities of the male punters in this chapter have all been changed), a forty-year-old factory worker:

'I am a single man living with my mother, I have lived at this address for all my life. I admit going to Cardiff to pick up a prostitute. I have been doing so for about two years, that's when I passed my test.'

And wonder what desperation presses a man to take his driving test at the age of forty, purely in order to obtain monthly sex in an industrial estate. But then it's easy to say that desperation is what drew everyone to the Custom House. Punters and prostitutes alike, what they had to declare in this particular Custom House was nothing less than their despair.

And mostly that would be true. Carol Richards, one of Lynette's numerous aunties, was interviewed by the police two days after the murder. First thing she said was, 'At the present time I'm heavily pregnant but I've still been going out to do business a couple of nights a week.'

One prostitute, explaining that she had badmouthed Lynette as an informant, added, 'But that was only because she used to try and get the police to arrest me rather than herself.' She went on to mention, 'The last time I worked as a prostitute was 23 January, which I remember because it was my birthday.'

Sharon Said's account of night on the beat: 'I was with two of my mates and Lynette White. We were all talking when suddenly I felt faint. Then I blacked out and collapsed on to the floor. The next thing I remember was waking up in the Cardiff Royal Infirmary. I was not aware how I got there until three days later . . . I have found the reason I collapsed was that I was going through the female menopause and it was affecting me.' Sharon Said was thirty-two at the time she made this statement.

By July she was talking to the police again, this time with another tale from the beat, one which she hoped might point to Lynette White's murderer. 'I was standing on the corner of Bute Street and Crichton Street when a man I now know to be Charlie Pritchard approached me, and I asked him if he wanted business. He said he did and he agreed he would pay £20 for a handjob. He gave the money to me and we walked across the road and into the alley behind the old Aspro Travel building. He unzipped his own trousers and I handed him a Durex which he placed on his penis. I started to masturbate him but he was unable to come. He then started to get stroppy and said to me, "You're all black men's trollops." He pushed me against the wall and he grabbed my throat with both hands. I shouted to a woman standing ten feet away. I told her to get the police . . . During the struggle Pritchard said to me, "Do you want to end up like the other fucking trollop?" In the months after the murder a lot of prostitutes came forward with similar stories from the front line. Among them was Angela Psaila, who, on 21 February, just a week after the murder, told the police about an incident from around six months earlier. 'I was working my beat in Riverside,' she said, ' when a man who I had never seen before pulled up in his car and asked for business . . . [the car] was light brown and had white striped furry seat covers. The driver was a white man in his thirties with dark brown short hair, very stocky and looked about six foot tall. I got in the car and directed him to Sophia Gardens.

'We went up to where the stables are in Pontcanna Fields. When we got there he gave me £10 which I always charge for sex in the car. I put a Durex on him and then he said he wanted it from behind. I knelt on the passenger seat facing the rear with my neck on the head rest. He was behind me and we started to have sex, he was unable to climax and I told him to take his penis out as I was getting cramp in my legs and my neck was aching. He started shouting at me and then the next thing I knew I was hit in the side of the face. I was very frightened of him and agreed for him to try again but he still couldn't climax. This had gone on for nearly an hour. I wanted to get away from him and so I said I was going to be sick. He then opened the car door and I managed to get out. He grabbed my arm and whilst holding me pushed a finger up my backside. I turned round and shouted at him and then managed to get away. I left my black patent handbag and green umbrella and black patent shoes in the car.'

But these war stories are not the whole story. Some of the Custom House prostitutes have surely been driven into the trade by cruel necessity, yet it seems unlikely that such women are even in the majority. The others earn good enough money and then piss it away as speedily as possible. Piss it away in the Custom House and the North Star, the Taurus Steak House and the Red Onion. And furthermore they enjoy pissing it away. Debbie Paul's description of the North Star Club before Lynette's death changed everything is hardly of a desolate place. To the uninitiated, the North Star looked less like your local branch of TGI Fridays than the hellhole at the end of the universe, but Debbie made a crucial distinction: just because ninety-nine per cent of the population wouldn't be seen dead in a particular place does not mean that the other one per cent are wrong in finding it entirely congenial – after all, the same applies to a no doubt lesser degree to the brand new opera house scheduled to be the jewel of the bay.

Likewise, while lamenting the brutal drudgery of the Custom House beat and being outraged at the behaviour of many of the punters, we should not forget the silent majority of punters, flushed out by this investigation, for whom the Custom House represents something like liberation. Punter after punter came up with statements to the effect that it wasn't sex they were interested in, they just wanted to talk to the girls. A cynical and immediate response is to assume that they're lying, vainly pleading a degree of innocence after being caught bang to rights, trying to cover up from their wives.

But a closer examination fails to confirm this theory. The married punters tend to be matter of fact: they may be lying about how often they visit prostitutes but they admit that their purpose was purely sexual – to be masturbated in the front seat of the car, or to fuck a girl bending over in an alleyway. There's little that's coy or even human about most of the marrieds. You're left with a vision of endless shoals of cold-eyed salesmen in bronze Granadas bearing down on the working girls of the world with their flies open and their wads at the ready.

The ones who say they only wanted to talk, though, most of them are approaching middle age and typically living with their mothers somewhere in the Valleys. As you read more and more statements you end up believing them, you're left with a clammy sense that our society really is so alienated that the company of the Custom House hustlers is the only company that this life's losers can find – these Valleys boys who've never had a girlfriend and are never going to have one. They are past forty and past hoping.

Like Norman Davies, forty-one at time of murder: 'I am a single man and I live with my parents. I have never been married and I am employed as a school caretaker. Prior to this I was unemployed and before that I had worked for twenty years, till I was made redundant.

'I can say that I have visited the Riverside red light area over the past two years at least and I normally park up and speak with the girls on the street. Just for a chat, I don't bother with the sex part of things. I have also used the Custom House in the Docks area of Cardiff and spoken to the prostitutes there in the past. With regard to Lynette White, I can say that I have never been with this young lady for sex, but I do believe I may have spoken to her in the street or the Custom House. I have seen this girl a few times around the streets of Cardiff as I have done the other girls. I would also like to add that I have never had sexual relationships with any of those girls. I know it sounds strange that I frequent the Docks area and visit the pubs and talk to the prostitutes but to be honest I enjoy being offered the services of the prostitutes and I like the prostitutes talking to me and it stimulates me sexually.'

And it's hard to imagine a bleaker alibi for the day after Lynette's murder than Norman's: 'On Sunday 14 February I was a bit fed up [because it had been raining too hard for him to go to the previous day's rugby match] so I went out in the car for a ride to pass the time way. I ended up in Ledbury, the other side of Hereford, and I decided to go to Birmingham on the train to pass some time away. I parked my car up at the railway station and I think I paid £3.90 for a ticket to Birmingham New Street Station. I think the train left Ledbury at around 3.45 p.m. and when I got to Birmingham I had a walk around and a cup of tea and I decided to get the next train back, which left at around 5.30 p.m. and I had to change trains at Malvern. When I got to Ledbury, around 7.30 p.m., I got in my car and drove home. I know this sounds a bit silly, but I get lonely. A Sunday is a long day to spend at home and I find it boring, to say the least.'

Then again, Norman Davies is maybe something of an extreme case. More typical perhaps is the younger and slightly more red-blooded Barry Evans, thirty-six at the time of the murder. 'I am a single man and live with my mother,' said Evans in his statement. 'For the past ten years I have visited the Cardiff area during the evenings . . . on occasions as much as three evenings a week . . . I spend some time around the Custom House and over a period of time have got to know most of the prostitutes. I have had intercourse with most of the girls there . . . I don't go for intercourse every time I visit the Custom House area, but have a talk to the girls.'

And did he know Lynette? 'It was during one of my visits to the Riverside area that I met Lynette White. I didn't know her as Lynette because she gave me some other name. She asked me if I wanted business and stated that the price outside was ten pounds. I don't own a car but have recently purchased a motor scooter. I agreed to her price and she took me to a lane at the back of the houses. Lynette produced a Durex for me to wear and we had intercourse with me standing behind her and she leaning forward. I spoke to her on a number of occasions after that, as I have the other prostitutes.'

If that doesn't provide a grim enough snapshot of Lynette's working life, then how about Mr Evans' next sexual encounter with Lynette. 'The room was very small and only contained a bed, a table and a settee. I remember Lynette switching on a two-bar electric fire as she said she was feeling cold. I think it was on this occasion that I had intercourse with Lynette that she had a black eye. I asked her what had happened and she said that her boyfriend did it because she wasn't giving him enough money. I didn't ask any more questions and never knew anything about her private life.'

None of these statements produced much of a clue as to who killed Lynette, but as slices of social documentary they are remarkable. A man called Geraint Williams (who incidentally proffers perhaps the finest non-alibi I've ever encountered: 'to be honest I was always drinking and taking speed and acid so I didn't know where I was half the time') mentions that the nearest he's ever been to the Docks was to visit an acquaintance called Tony, 'I met him in prison, I believe he was doing time for neglecting his children who died in the bath.'

Reading these statements I found myself hoping that they were in no way typical, that life couldn't be so cruel, or society so unsafe. But I am left with the sense that they are all too typical. Many of these statements repeatedly pulled the rug from under me. Until I am forced to acknowledge that this place we live in is not nice and not safe.

And so 1988 was slipping by with the police getting nowhere until, nine months after the murder, a couple of clues turned up. The first was the apparently innocuous statement to the police by a woman named Violet Perriam, a receptionist at the Butetown Health Centre. The second was the rape of Angela Psaila.

Whilst out on the beat Psaila picked a wrong punter. He raped and beat her on waste ground around the corner from the Custom House. Psaila went to the police and in the course of the investigation they took a blood test from her.

Of more immediate interest to the police, however, was Violet Perriam's evidence. On 10 November she made a statement to the police that she had been driving home along James Street at 1.30 a.m. on the night of the murder. As she drove she noticed a knot of four men standing outside the bookie's apparently arguing amongst themselves. In this initial statement she simply said that a couple of the men looked familiar to her from having seen them in the Health Centre. But on 16 November she made a second statement and this time she positively identified one of these men as Rashid Omar; she went on to speculate that another was John Actie. 'I didn't see his face,' she said, 'but he is a very big person and stands out because of his description. He was wearing a black leather jacket which he always wears.'

Now this was of real interest to the police. Next step was to attempt to corroborate this sighting. They called in for questioning those parties who might have spotted something going on in James Street: specifically Angela Psaila, whose St Clare's Court flat offered a view of that section of James Street, and Mark Grommek, who lived upstairs and must surely have noticed any disturbance.

On 17 November they pulled in Psaila. Most of the people involved in the case barely knew Angela Psaila: Stephen Miller still has trouble remembering her name, John Actie had never even heard of her, Yusef Abdullahi – Dullah – likewise knew nothing of her. Those that did know her, though, are considerably less than enthusiastic. Tony Paris has made it his business to know every female resident in Butetown and had actually had sex with Angela, but describes the encounter in spectacularly brutal terms: 'She's the most horrible fucking monster I've ever seen, you wouldn't want to be close to her in a darkened room. But sometimes, when the mood takes you . . . it was a case of any port in a storm.'

The single exception from amongst the ranks of the defendants seems to be Ronnie Actie, who knew Angela through having been Leanne's boyfriend. Ronnie provides one of the few moments of comedy available amongst the acres of police transcripts when DC Haines asks him what he made of Angela, whether he thought she was a hard girl and Ronnie says no, she seemed a very nice, very soft girl. Haines is transparently flabbergasted by this.

The police finally started to get somewhere when they questioned Psaila, who told them that on the night of the murder she had indeed seen several men in James Street outside number seven: Stephen Miller, John Actie, Ronnie Actie, Dullah and Tony Brace. Then Stephen Miller came up to her flat looking for Lynette. Psaila told him that she wasn't there, and Miller left. Psaila then looked out of the window and saw Miller meet up with John Actie before walking out on to James Street to meet Ronnie Actie. John then stood by the door to number seven, and Miller and Ronnie walked up and down. After a while Ronnie shouted up at the second-floor flat (described by Psaila as 'where the two gays live'), where there was a light on. Eventually a man came down and let Ronnie in. While Ronnie was inside screams were heard but John Actie and Miller remained outside, where they were joined by a taxi driven by Jack Ellis, and by Tony Paris who she described as moving to and fro selling ganja. After an hour or so Miller and John left in the taxi with Jack Ellis, Tony Paris disappeared, and ten minutes later Ronnie Actie re-emerged from the flat.

It's a somewhat garbled and confusing account that bears every sign of being improvised on the hoof, but it gave the police a few more names to work with. Chief amongst these names were Mark Grommek and Paul Atkins, the 'two gays' from the upstairs flat.

Grommek and Atkins, two gay men now in their thirties, are the odd couple trapped at the centre of this case. Grommek, who was in the flat above that in which Lynette White was murdered, was one of the first people the police interviewed. He didn't help his own cause by starting off with a collection of mostly rather pointless lies. Clearly nervous, he prattled on about spending most of his time with seventy-year-old Betty Donovan, even claiming that he used to go out with her to the Red Dragon bar – Cardiff's least inviting gay bar. As for what he was doing at the time of the murder he simply claims to have been asleep and, in a later statement, to have taken sleeping pills.

The police steadily unravelled Grommek's fictions and when they discovered that he had not been alone at all but in the company of Paul Atkins, suspicion turned firmly on to the pair of them. This suspicion was swiftly amplified by rumours that swept the community. A typical homosexual killing, was the gossipmongers' verdict for a while – conveniently ignoring the fact that most victims of 'typical homosexual killings' are homosexual men, not women. But still, anti-gay prejudice was and is strong enough for there still to be people who'll swear that Grommek and Atkins must be the real murderers.

They're not a greatly prepossessing pair these two. Grommek, in particular, with his foxy features and scraggy blond moustache would be typecast as the low-life spiv that his record reveals him to be – three years' imprisonment in London for attempted armed robbery with a replica pistol, ten months' borstal for stealing a £5 jacket, on probation for shoplifting at the time of the murder, and using a different name to the one under which he acquired his criminal record – Mark Taylor. Atkins, meanwhile, is a shorter, stockier figure with a certain air of innocence contrasting with Grommek's shiftiness. Atkins was judged to be of limited intelligence, is certainly unable to read or write, and, like Grommek, he's a petty criminal who has served time in prison.

The world that they both lived in was Cardiff's gay scene. Like Cardiff's lesbian scene, the male gay scene is neither glamorous nor politicized but the province of working-class outsiders. And, again like the lesbian scene and unlike the gay scene in larger metropolises, it is not an exclusive scene. That's to say, it has to share much of its territory with other outsiders: lesbians, prostitutes – or the unholy coalition of 'lesbians, pimps, queers, prostitutes, ship guys' that Debbie Paul identified as frequenting the North Star.

The focus of Cardiff's gay scene is around a handful of bars and clubs towards the southern end of the town centre. There's the Red Dragon bar, next to the train station; the King's Cross pub, just a few hundred yards to the east, at the top of Caroline Street; and, round the corner from the King's Cross, there's Tunnels club in the cul de sac that offers service access to the St Mary Street Arcade. A few years ago you could have added to this list, the Golden Cross pub, for prostitutes and people who just didn't care; Sirs at the Terminus, for gay men; Barrels Wine Bar, for lesbians; and Hunters Club in the Oxford Arcade; all of which have closed down or changed identity in the name of regeneration.

This was the gay scene that Grommek and Atkins were a part of, lived in – not a Greenwich Village world of leather bars and S&M *boîtes* but a mundane circuit of drab bars interspersed with endless treks to meet so-and-so for yet another aimless cup of tea en route to nowhere in particular, and only the odd illicit half-hour spent in the bus station toilets or the Castle grounds to add a faint gloss of danger to the life.

On 22 November, following Angela Psaila's statement that he had opened the door to Ronnie Actie, the police re-arrested Mark Grommek. For four hours Grommek stuck to his guns, but by five o'clock he changed his story decisively. He admitted that he had not been alone that night. A friend, Paul Atkins, had called on him at around 12.30 a.m. This perhaps explains Psaila's otherwise confusing reference to the two gays, Grommek being the sole tenant. It lends a little credibility to the Psaila account. Then Grommek went further.

At around 1.30 a.m., he told the police, his doorbell rang again, and he went down to open the door, only to find four men standing there: Dullah, Ronnie Actie, a white guy called Martin Tucker and an unknown tall black man with shoulder-length dreadlocks and a slight beard, a goatee maybe. Dullah asked if anyone was in Flat One, to which Grommek replied, 'Not as far as I know,' and went back upstairs, leaving the door open. Back in the flat Grommek told Atkins what had happened and then they heard raised voices in the flat below, followed by some horrible screams. When everything had become quiet, Atkins went downstairs, came back, told Grommek that there was a murdered girl downstairs and was promptly sick. Atkins remained in the flat till early morning and then Grommek went to sleep.

Now things were moving apace for the police. That same evening Paul Atkins was called in. Atkins was already well known to the police, having previous convictions and having already made statements in this case. He was interviewed by DCI John Ludlow on 10 April 1988. On this occasion he made a bizarre statement which started off by admitting that he was in the upstairs flat with Mark Grommek at the time of the murder. Then he went on to accuse a gay man called Barry from Bristol of having committed the murder. When pushed for details he changed the story to make it Grommek who carried out the murder, with Grommek emerging from the murder room, carrying a bloodstained knife and saying, 'I done her for the money, I had £45.' Further questioning, however, caused Atkins to change his story once again. This time he confessed that it was he who had killed her; he said that he'd met Lynette in the Custom House, asked her for sex, gone back to James Street and then stabbed her. At this point, not before time, Atkins admitted that he was telling lies.

Atkins's suggestibility to police questioning, then, would be hard to overestimate. Anyway he provided partial corroboration for Grommek's tale. He admitted to being at the flat, said he heard a group of men outside arguing and that the doorbell rang and Grommek went to answer, looking upset when he returned. Then he heard the argument and the screams and went down to see what had happened.

At this point Atkins's account diverges from Grommek's. He says he saw a white girl with dark hair in a pony tail climbing the stairs and together they discovered the body. The girl, whose description clearly matches that of Leanne Vilday, then said that she knew the victim and would go to the police. Atkins went back upstairs, told Grommek, and left in the early morning.

Meanwhile Psaila was still being questioned. She offered nothing new until – perhaps after being confronted with Atkins's statement – she finally admitted that Leanne Vilday had not been out of the St Clare's Court flat, as she had previously claimed, but had been there all the time and had indeed gone over to the murder flat after the screams, to see what had happened, so discovering Lynette's body.

Now, at last, the police had a solid basis upon which to call in Leanne Vilday, the woman they had long suspected of knowing more than she was telling. On 6 December they brought her in for questioning, along with Psaila, Grommek and Atkins.

Angela Psaila merely refined her tale, bringing Dullah into the centre of the action. On the night of the murder, she reiterated, Stephen Miller had come to her flat looking for Lynette. On learning that she wasn't there, Miller then left the flat and, as Angela observed from her lounge window, met John Actie in the car park below. The two men then walked out on to James Street, where they met Ronnie Actie, Yusef Abdullahi and Tony Paris. After a while Psaila then saw John Actie talking to someone leaning out of the second-floor window at 7 James Street, following which conversation the street door was opened from the inside.

At this point some of the men, John Actie and Miller probably, left in a car and Ronnie Actie and Dullah went into the building. Shortly afterwards screams could be heard and Leanne, who had just returned to St Clare's Court, decided to go and see what was happening, while Angela remained at home. A little later Leanne returned and reported that Lynette had been stabbed to death. Leanne stayed for a while, had a bath, and then left the flat at around 3 a.m. Miller then returned to the flat, made an ambiguous threat and left. Angela finally went to bed, only to hear John Actie's voice saying, 'Open up, I know you're in there,' but she kept quiet. Actie left, and that was that for the night.

Meanwhile, Leanne Vilday started to talk, and her tale turned out to be significantly different to Psaila's but uncannily similar to Grommek's. By her account she was putting the rubbish out when she heard the screams from James Street. She looked out from her balcony and saw that the door to 7 James Street was open, with Ronnie Actie's green Cortina parked outside. Leanne ran over the road and into 7 James Street. She climbed the stairs and saw Martin Tucker stood by the flat door. Inside the flat she saw Ronnie Actie standing by the bedroom door and, inside the room, Lynette lying dead on the floor surrounded by Stephen Miller, Yusef Abdullahi and an unknown black man with shoulder-length dreadlocks. Leanne then ran out, returned to Angela's, didn't tell Angela what had happened, but went to the bathroom and then left to meet Ronnie Actie at the North Star just before 3.30 a.m., closing time.

Grommek and Atkins had little to add to their earlier stories. Violet Perriam's statement too was slotted into the police's patchwork and Rashid Omar was added to the list of possible killers – perhaps suspected of being the unknown black guy reported by Vilday and Grommek.

Next step for the police was to round up this extensive cast of characters. Angela Psaila's various statements had by now implicated Ronnie Actie, John Actie, Stephen Miller, Yusef Abdullahi, Tony Brace and Tony Paris; Grommek and Vilday had added in Martin Tucker, and Perriam pointed towards Rashid Omar.

Meanwhile the police were far from finished with their star witnesses, none of whom, at this stage, showed much sign of having told the whole truth and nothing but the truth. The interrogations continued.

On 7 December arrests were made. Within the next couple of days Martin Tucker and Tony Brace were alibied. Rashid Omar was so marginally implicated and remained so steadfastly silent under interrogation, that the police had no alternative but to let him go. Interestingly enough, with Omar's departure from the questioning, the unknown black man with the goatee also made a speedy disappearance from Vilday's future statements.

Then, on 10 December, Stephen Miller cracked. The ice man from Brixton, the cocaine pimp, proved himself under interrogation to have the IQ of an eleven-year-old, and not that much more in the way of street smarts when it came to handling this kind of harsh prolonged questioning.

From his eighth statement onwards, after three days in custody, Miller began to confess. He made, with considerable assistance from the police officers interviewing him, the subsequently retracted statement that was used to damn him in court. This was an account of the murder broadly similar to Vilday's except for the fact that Miller replaced Tucker and the unknown dread with Tony Paris and two white guys.

On 11 December the police reckoned they'd hit the jackpot. Someone thought to check the blood taken from Angela Psaila after her rape against the bloodstains found on Lynette's jeans and, presto, they had a match. Angela Psaila's blood belonged to the group AB:PGM+1-:EAP B/CB:Hp2:Gc2- 1S:AK1, a group that only one in thirty-eight hundred belong to.

No longer was Psaila going to be allowed to get away with saying she'd never been over to 7 James Street herself. Psaila now told the police that, on hearing the screams from 7 James Street, she had in fact accompanied Leanne over the road. They saw Dullah and Ronnie Actie enter the building.

Following them inside, they encountered John Actie standing at the top of the stairs. They pushed past him and entered the room hot on the heels of Dullah and Ronnie. There they found Tony Paris attacking Lynette with Stephen Miller and – a new arrival – his brother Tony Miller watching. From here on Psaila's story stays more or less the same, except for the fact that she places Tony Miller in the midst of the action.

Vilday was confronted with this new evidence and now she too remembered that Angela had, after all, been there and that she had been mistaken in alleging that Martin Tucker and an unknown black guy were among the gang, but remembered that, in fact, John Actie and Tony Paris were there instead.

At last, the police had a story. There were holes, of course. For instance, no one even pretends to know what happened to Lynette White between the Wednesday when Stephen Miller dropped her off on the beat and the Saturday night when she was killed. It's just generally supposed that she was hiding out at the flat in 7 James Street, where she was eventually killed.

There were, however, numerous reported sightings of Lynette during this period. The most plausible of these are from fellow prostitutes who say they saw her on the beat over in Riverside. Less convincing are reports, generally from people who didn't know her but had seen her face in the papers, that she was seen in assorted city centre nightclubs. Most tantalizing is a claim, made by a somewhat unreliable witness named Ronnie Williams, that Lynette was seen in a white car with several out-of-town black guys in the City Road area.

In the absence of any substantiated alternative theory, though, we may as well assume that Lynette was based in James Street. The one incontrovertible fact is that that was where she ended up that Saturday night. And it's what happened there that night that was the crux of the police investigation.

The story that finally satisfied the police from all the hours of questioning Mark Grommek, Paul Atkins, Leanne Vilday and Angela Psaila, and was backed up by the confession of Stephen Miller himself, goes as follows. On Saturday night, 13 February, the rumour got back to Miller that Lynette had been at Angela's flat, St Clare's Court, all the time. So he returned to the flat that night demanding to see her. Angela sent him away.

Miller returned to the Casablanca Club's Valentine's Dance to hear the sweeter-than-sugar sounds of Sandra Cross, a lover's rock singer, but he was still a long way from giving up the hunt. Instead, on his reappearance at the Casablanca, Miller somehow got the word that Lynette was at 7 James Street, perhaps from Ronnie Actie, Leanne's part-time boyfriend.

A group of men then gathered around Miller, taunting him with the suggestion that he was not man enough to keep hold of a woman, even a cheap hustler like Lynette. If I were you I'd teach her a lesson, they said. C'mon man let's sort her out, make her show some respect.

And so, out of the drink-and-drugged-up atmosphere of the Saturday night Casa crowd, a lynch party was born. Miller and Ronnie Actie plus the little guy who cleared up the glasses at the Club, Tony Paris, and the big guy who watched the door, John Actie, headed off towards the James Street flat, no more than fifty yards away, just above the bookie's. Along the way they somehow picked up Yusef Abdullahi, who had returned unexpectedly from his job, working through the weekend on a ship ten miles away in Barry. Maybe he was en route to the Casa from the North Star where his mate Ronnie Williams swore he'd seen him during the course of the evening.

Arriving at the flat they rang the doorbell. The bell for Flat One. No reply. Then they waited around for ten minutes before ringing the bell for Flat Two. Eventually Mark Grommek, the flat's tenant, came down and let the men in. They then bundled into the flat, Lynette having presumably opened the door to them. And trouble started almost immediately – the surprising leader of the attack being Tony Paris, physically by far the least forceful of the five, and the only one without a known capacity for violence.

Tony Paris went berserk on entering the front bedroom of 7 James Street, the only room habitable at the time as the electricity was cut off and this room was illuminated by the streetlights outside. So Tony went for Lynette with the knife and she screamed.

Her scream was then heard by Angela Psaila and Leanne Vilday back in the St Clare's Court flat, over the road from James Street. With remarkable acuity and striking public spiritedness they decided that the faint screams came from the James Street flat and, without pausing, they hurried over the road to help, leaving behind Leanne's baby, Craig.

Having crossed the road, they were able to push open the front door to 7 James Street. They then went up the stairs and ran into John Actie standing in the doorway. Despite the fact that John Actie is a very large man, and the doorway on the small side, not to mention the fact that John Actie is regularly employed for the express purpose of stopping unwanted people going through doors; despite all that, these two women just pushed past him, turned right and went down the corridor to the front room, while John Actie remained in the corridor and took no further part in matters.

Once inside, they encountered Tony Paris hitting a struggling Lynette. Angela rushed to Lynette's assistance only to be grabbed by Abdullahi and Ronnie Actie, who held her from behind and slapped her face, drawing blood. At this point Stephen Miller stabbed Lynette three times while Tony Paris held her down on the bed. Lynette fell to the floor, moaning; she tried to get up, got her hands on to the windowsill but fell back to the floor. Angela stopped watching but could hear Lynette being stabbed some more. Then Miller came over to Angela, put a knife to her back and forced her to cut Lynette's wrist with another knife. Miller proceeded to threaten Angela and Leanne with a knife to their throats, and told them to keep their mouths shut. The two of them then returned to the St Clare's Court flat, where Angela took off her bloody top and put it in the bin, and Leanne waited for an hour or so before deciding, at 3.20 a.m., to nip over to the North Star for a quick drink before closing and to meet Ronnie Actie, her part-time boyfriend and now murderer of her best friend, with whom she would spend the remainder of the night.

At least that's Angela's account of the actual murder. In fact what the police really had was not one story but two. Leanne Vilday's is significantly different to Angela's. By her account she was actually in the courtyard of the flats, putting the rubbish out, when she heard the scream. She returned to the flat, recruited Angela, went into 7 James Street and pushed past John Actie. Actie, in this version, followed the two women into the front room and shut the door behind them. Lynette was already apparently dead by the time they arrived in the room, lying inert on the floor. Miller then decided to force Leanne to cut Lynette's wrist. John Actie made Leanne go through with this, holding a knife to her throat. Then Angela was forced to follow suit. Next Leanne was asked to cut Lynette's throat. She refused and meanwhile Tony Paris decided to stab Lynette some more. At which point Leanne and Angela left. Angela then removed her bloodstained clothing and Leanne went off to the North Star to meet Ronnie Actie.

The two accounts show discrepancies, surely enough, but maybe these could be due to the extraordinary trauma of stumbling upon such a scene of mayhem. No wonder, perhaps, that Angela reckons John Actie never entered the room, while Leanne remembers him holding her at knifepoint. Nothing impossible, then, in Angela remembering Lynette as alive and kicking, while Leanne saw her prostrate and dead.

SIX

The Trial: A World Turned Upside Down

And so the case came to trial. Of course there was much that had been done beforehand. Both sides had scurried around preparing their cases. The defence lawyers – in particular Leila Attfield and Stuart Hutton of Huttons, David Webster of Abse, Cohen and Bernard De Maid of De Maid and De Maid – tried to find potential alibi witnesses, while the police kept their main witnesses as far out of things as possible.

The police still had work to do. The confession they had could only legally be used against Miller, and the evidence of Vilday, Psaila, Grommek and Atkins was liable to look a little shaky under cross-examination. So they went out looking for corroboration. Putting pressure on the friends and family had some success in Dullah's case, as we shall see. But getting anyone to corroborate the allegations against John, Ronnie and Tony was a harder matter.

In fact they never did succeed in finding anyone to implicate John or Ronnie but something certainly did crop up with regard to Tony. Tony was on remand in Cardiff Prison and one of the inmates on the same block was a fella called Ian Massey. Massey was a helpful sort of chap who seemed to know his way around the system, and he offered to take a look at Tony's papers and see if he could think of anything that might help. Tony thought that was fine.

Just a day before the trial was due to start he discovered that it wasn't fine at all. Massey turned out to have told the police that Tony had confessed to him, and he proceeded to give the police an account of this confession that dovetailed marvellously neatly with the evidence given by the various prosecution witnesses. So the police went in to the trial with an ace already on the table.

The defence too had a difficult job. Finding authoritative witnesses who could nail down precisely what time it was that they might have seen Ronnie or John or Tony in the Casablanca Club, a year or so previously, was always liable to be a fairly fruitless task.

Stephen Miller, for a start, had little in the way of an alibi: he simply says he went to the Valentines' Dance at the Casablanca, was mostly in the company of Pepsi Orton, but left for a while to look for Lynette at the North Star Club, passing 7 James Street on his way to and from the North Star. Orton confirms this, but obviously doesn't provide a watertight alibi.

Ronnie Actie was little better off. He also went to the Casablanca on his habitual Saturday night round of pubs, pool hall and clubs in the company of his mate and after the Casablanca closed he went on his own to the North Star Club where Leanne met him at around 3.30 in the morning. His mate was unable to provide a useful alibi because he was unable to distinguish, nine months later, that particular Saturday night from any other, and was anyway rather hampered as a defence witness by an unfortunate previous conviction (for perjury). Vilday, however, does at least agree with Ronnie about the matter of meeting him in the North Star.

John Actie and Tony Paris had slightly more solid stories. They were both working in the Casablanca that night, John on the door and Tony collecting glasses. The manager and other staff are all sure that neither could have stopped work for more than a few minutes without being missed. But the police – while never disputing that the two men were working that night – still maintain that they were both lured away from their posts by the chance to band together with a group of people who were not their friends and go murder a prostitute. Furthermore the police maintain that both these men were able to take part in this ferocious murder, undergoing a complete change of character in Paris's case, and still return to work minutes afterwards without so much as a bloodstain upon them and without betraying to their workmates any hint of the horror they'd immersed themselves in.

Ordinarily both Paris's and Actie's alibi evidence might be seen as fairly substantial. The problem was that the Casablanca's staff were mostly black men with criminal records and the defence knew that the police might be able to imply that they were a bunch of liars who would provide alibis for the brothers, wouldn't they.

Yusef Abdullahi thought his alibi was rock solid. He had spent the weekend of the murder working on a ship, the *Coral Sea*, in Barry Docks, ten miles or so from Butetown. Once again the police do not dispute this, but claim that he must have left the ship for a few hours, late on Saturday night and by some unspecified means of transport (there being no public transport and Yusef not possessing a vehicle of his own), headed for the Butetown clubs, fallen in with the murderous posse somewhere between the Casablanca and the James Street flat, taken full part in the killing, and then returned to the boat, again by unspecified means, where his workmates also failed to notice either his absence or anything in his behaviour or appearance that might suggest he had recently stepped out of a bloodbath.

Against this police account Abdullahi found at least thirteen witnesses to say he was on the boat all the time. Nor were these men all easily marginalized as a bunch of brothers from Butetown; they were a disparate group of labourers from Cardiff and Liverpool, only one or two of whom had ever met Abdullahi before. The police, however, responded to this apparent hiccup in their case by systematically reinterviewing these witnesses about this weekend nine months previous until they became uncertain as to whether such-and-such an event happened on the Saturday or the Sunday night, what time it was precisely when they saw Dullah, and so on. They succeeded in making what should have been a cast-iron alibi look shaky. To take a typical example: at one point a co-worker, Les McCarthy, was persuaded to say that he had dropped Dullah into Cardiff on the Saturday night, before cross-checking made him certain that it must have been the Sunday. Other witnesses, like Bryn Samuel, became so fed up with repeated questioning that they stopped cooperating with the police, and this point was never pressed by the defence in court.

A further blow was struck to Dullah's credibility when his associate Ronnie Williams claimed that he had seen Dullah in the North Star late on the Saturday night. Williams has since acknowledged that he is actually far from sure which Saturday it was that he saw Dullah in the North Star – after all they both went there regularly – but by then the damage had been done, he'd testified in court.

Still, though, the defence case looked solid. Even if one accepted that all the alibis were more or less bogus, one was still left with a rather implausible scenario: two men who were not friends but who both had relationships with prostitutes – Ronnie Actie and Stephen Miller – met up in the Casablanca Club, where they persuaded two other men, who they knew but did not associate with – John Actie and Tony Paris – to leave their work and come and teach a lesson to a girl that John Actie, at least, didn't even know. On the way there they bumped into Yusef Abdullahi, an associate of Ronnie Actie but an enemy of John Actie, who was skyving off work in Barry, presumably in search of a good time, and he promptly agreed to join in. Then, having committed the murder, one man went to meet a woman who he'd attempted to force into becoming an accessory to the murder, in order to take her back to his sister's place. Two others went back to work at the Casablanca and a fourth to work in Barry without any of them leaving a trace.

And even if the alibi evidence for the defence was not convincing enough, the forensic evidence should have been overwhelming. No forensic evidence whatsoever links any of the five men accused of Lynette White's murder to the scene of the crime. Forensic reports suggest that, apart from Lynette White's own blood, there was one other person's blood found on the wall, and one person's blood on the jeans. The analysis of the blood on the jeans is more sophisticated. These blood-stains have been precisely identified as being from a rare combination of blood groups possessed by around one in thirty-eight hundred of the population. The blood on the wall is more vaguely identified, yielding only the less specific information that it belongs to type AB, possessed by one in six of the population and compatible with the blood on the jeans. Therefore it seems likely enough that all the blood comes from one person, that is, the murderer.

The apparently crucial discovery was that this rare blood type precisely matched Angela Psaila's blood. Otherwise the only potentially significant piece of information was that Abdullahi's blood is type AB and could therefore match the blood on the wall, though not on the jeans. The overwhelming likelihood, though, seemed to be that this was Angela Psaila's blood.

Then the forensic case fell apart. Chromosome sampling of five separate bloodstains on the jeans reveals male Y chromosomes every time. The police attempted to retain their breakthrough by positing that this might be due to Psaila having some of Yusef Abdullahi's type AB blood on her hands. However the forensics experts, Hayward & Co, called in by the defence pointed out that the likelihood of five separate stains being made up of a combination of two people's blood is frankly minimal. Further damage to the police case was then done by the DNA testing. The bloodstains from the jeans were found to have deteriorated too badly for effective testing. The stains on the wall, though, gave a partial result that was enough to eliminate all the suspects, including both Psaila and Abdullahi.

So in the end the forensics led nowhere. The police were unable to find a single bloodstain or fingerprint belonging to any of the five men they alleged had packed themselves into this small dark room. Yet the few days in December when they appeared to have clear evidence that Angela Psaila was in that room gave the police time and leverage enough to elicit the statements they wanted. Most likely, a freakish coincidence relating to Psaila's blood led directly to her confession. However, it should not be forgotten that even though the one-in-thirty-eight-hundred test was only in effect a part of a larger test which included two further levels – sex and DNA – Psaila's match was treated as a jackpot by the police.

Without forensic support the police case relied almost entirely on the alleged eyewitness statements of Vilday, Psaila, Grommek and Atkins, as well as the confession of Stephen Miller. But here, too, there were ample grounds for the defence to raise objections. For a start, nothing casts more doubt on the truthfulness of these statements than the remarkable fluctuations in the names of those accused of being in on the murder – around fifteen different names being mentioned at one time or another.

And if the central plank of the prosecution – the identification by independent witnesses of the five accused – was washed away, then all the defence had to worry about was the matter of Stephen Miller's conviction. Stephen Miller claims that his confession was made as a result of relentless police pressure, and was a complete fabrication. As for his apparent inside knowledge of the crime, he maintains that the police led him through it by the nose.

The following extract from his confession, in which he's getting down to the nitty-gritty of the crime, makes his point eloquently enough:

DC MURRAY: Is the bed central, or to the rear of the room or nearer the window?

MILLER: I can't be really . . . it was in between . . . I am sure she dropped to her left, but I could be mistaken, as I say it was dark, and I was out of my head . . . I can't be sure if she dropped right or left, but I am positive she dropped left . . .

DC MURRAY: If I say when the body was discovered the bed was in fact to the rear of the room on that wall? From the forensic evidence . . . where you have said the body has fallen, and where you have said the attack has taken place, it doesn't seem to ring true. I am not saying you haven't told the truth to the best of your ability but let's try. Let's try and see if we have got things wrong.

MILLER: It was dark ... I can't really be certain if the attack took place in the middle, the left or the right ... But I know she was on the floor.

DC MURRAY: We are not uh doubting that. The forensic evidence would suggest the body was elsewhere. I am saying that because it has to be brought up. Could you be mistaken as to where some of the injuries were inflicted? Could there be a movement from where she fell, to where some injuries were inflicted?

MILLER: Most probably, because it was dark.

DC MURRAY: So she could have crawled around?

MILLER: I couldn't be sure, she might have crawled into the corner or something, I just don't know.

DC MURRAY: So without giving too much away to you ... because I don't want to tell you the scene, so that you can describe it as a result of me telling you ...

MILLER: I understand.

DC MURRAY: OK, it would appear that some injuries have been inflicted at the end of the bed, as opposed to along the side of the bed ... Now, does that ring any bells?

MILLER: I don't know, not as far as I know ...

DC MURRAY: Do you remember there being curtains?

MILLER: I don't remember nothing ...

DC EVANS: Was anybody behind Leanne when she came in?

MILLER: Uh, most possible, I can't say.

DC MURRAY: I'll just clarify exactly what that was ... you have made yourself clear but we will get it all in a nice little package, all right.

The first trial started a year after the initial arrests. It was held before Mr Justice MacNeill. Eighty-two days later the evidence had all been heard, and Justice MacNeill was about to begin his summing up, when he died of a heart attack.

Three months later, in May 1990, the second trial began. It was heard by Mr Justice Leonard and held, like the first trial, in Swansea, West Glamorgan, because of fears that there might be attempts at intimidation and public disturbances if the trial were heard in Cardiff.

Yet, while Swansea is less than fifty miles from Cardiff geographically speaking, temperamentally it's a world away. Swansea is a small, placid coastal town, a city in name alone. It's a much more identifiably Welsh city than Cardiff, and also a very much whiter place than Cardiff. If Cardiff's the cosmopolitan, commercial capital of enterprise-zone Wales, Swansea is the repository of the principality's traditional values, a non-conformist chapel town. All of which made it a hard town for the defence. An all-white Swansea jury was confronted with five black men from Cardiff, from Tiger Bay even, that fabled den of big-city iniquity. It would certainly be unfair to say that they were found guilty before the trial started – Swansea is hardly the deep South – but the racial and geographical origins of the accused cannot have exactly helped their chances.

In the key speech of the epic 115-day trial the prosecutor for the crown, Mr David Elfer, made ample use of those innate South Walian prejudices. 'Butetown', he said, 'is an upside-down society.' It's a place, he said, where people carry knives as a matter of routine, where terrible acts of violence, he implied, are no more than commonplace. The effect of this speech was simple and deadly. Suddenly it was not simply these five men who were on trial for this particular murder, it was Butetown that was on trial for having an evil reputation. And, in the final analysis, that was no great distance from an American defence lawyer telling an all-white jury that the lone black man named Rodney King, who appeared on videotape to be undergoing a terrible beating at the hands of a whole bunch of cops, was actually provoking and threatening them. No great distance in the end from asking the jury if they would like to be alone in a dark Butetown alley with these five black men.

104

Mr Elfer, of course, never explicitly raised such a
motion. It was left to Angela Psaila to do that. In the n
of her spectacularly incoherent – even by her own stan
– testimony, she suddenly railed at the defendants, called them
black bastards and fucking monkeys.

The prosecution witnesses were terrible: the new witnesses,
Harris, Williams et al, were basically flimsy; Grommek and
Atkins were laughably bad; and Vilday and Psaila little better.
They contradicted themselves and each other. They could
never even agree a definitive line-up of who was in the murder
room, Angela repeatedly insisting that Tony Miller was there
too. In fact they were so bad that when it came to the sum-
ming-up, Mr Justice Leonard warned the jury that it would
be unsafe to convict simply on the words of Vilday and Psaila.

So when the jury eventually went out, nearly six months
after the trial had started, things were looking good for Ronnie
and John Actie: the only evidence against them was from
Vilday and Psaila, no one else, not even Miller in his confession, had implicated them at all. Nor were things looking
too bad for Abdullahi and Paris: all they had against them
were the frankly dubious testimonies of Yusef's common-law
wife, Jackie Harris, and the grass Ian Massey. Of course they
were implicated by Miller in his confession, but that shouldn't
have mattered. Miller was in the hardest corner: he had his
confession to live down and had at least some kind of a motive,
which was more than the others could boast. It's not, on the
face of it, the most convincing of confessions. But once again
it came out of the course of a bewildering number of interviews.
And its very muddled incoherence may have made an impact
on the jury that the defence failed to neutralize.

After many hours of deliberation the jury's foreman came
out and requested the chance to listen to a section of Tape 14
one more time. This was a section of the tape in which a
semi-hysterical Miller can be heard babbling about Tony Paris
stabbing and stabbing and stabbing. Shortly afterwards, they
came out with their first verdicts.

The verdict was spread over two days, so difficult was it for them to agree even then, and by the time it was finished the jury members were tearful and exhausted. On the first day Stephen Miller and Tony Paris were found guilty while Ronnie Actie was acquitted. On the second day John Actie was freed and Yusef Abdullahi found guilty.

The scenes that followed were extraordinary – not the scenes that surrounded the three found guilty, they were led off in familiar fashion, shouting their innocence at the TV cameras – but the scenes that surrounded the two acquittals. Something like a frenzy enveloped the Acties as they were released. Particularly on the second day when Ronnie was there to escort John away, the two of them were suddenly at the centre of a clan of crop-headed brothers and cousins who simply radiated the purest rage at the system that had locked them up. There was a palpable sense of defiance and anger such that it was easy to believe that they might have broken John out of the jailhouse had he not been acquitted. And at the centre of all this was John and his face was something to behold. He looked as if he might explode from the weight of powerful and conflicting emotions – exultation, hatred, fear, relief, despair and nervous exhaustion all there, all at the same time. A man about to cry tears of blood.

And then they piled into a convoy of flash motors and hightailed it out of wild West Glamorgan.

The longest murder trial in British legal history was over. And Stephen Miller and Yusef Abdullahi and Tony Paris were sentenced to life in prison. And the police had a party.

SEVEN

Unwrapping the Package: the Case for the Defence

From a distance it appeared that justice had been done. The newspapers, for instance, swallowed it without a problem. Five very bad guys, black gangsters and pimps, had gathered together, no doubt under the influence of drugs, and brutally murdered a white woman, a common prostitute who presumably must have ripped one of them off, or otherwise done them down. After all, that's the sort of thing that the law-abiding masses suspect must happen with crack-crazed underworld types, in the black ghettos of our cities.

It even carried some conviction with those who fancied they knew more than the general public: local newspaper reporters, community leaders, and so on. After all, John Actie's name has long been associated with the shady side of Butetown; Abdullahi too was a drug dealer; and as for Miller, well, it's simply common sense to look at the pimp when a prostitute gets killed.

To a Swansea jury, the accused – John Actie, Ronnie Actie, Yusef Abdullahi, Tony Paris and Stephen Miller – may have looked like a cohesive bunch, all tarred with the same brush, but take even a little time to find out more and it becomes clear that this would have been a very strange bunch of people to find having a drink together, let alone conspiring in a killing. The closer you look at this picture, the less convincing it seems.

Even John and Ronnie Actie are considerably less closely connected than was generally assumed. For a start, they are cousins not brothers. They grew up in different areas of the city, John in Llanrumney and Ronnie in Gabalfa, and while

John moved to Butetown, Ronnie still lives out to the north of the city. Even inasmuch as they have both been involved in various forms of villainy, they have nevertheless been rather different kinds of villain. Compared to John, Ronnie is just a hand-to-mouth hustler. Added to that, John has little fondness for the company of white people, and despises the prostitutes and hustlers that Ronnie hung out with. So while the cousins certainly knew each other and were on good enough terms, they were hardly close. For similar reasons John had little to do with Stephen Miller, and the only blood between him and Dullah was bad blood. As for Lynette White, he maintains he never even knew her name while she was alive.

Ronnie Actie, Stephen Miller and Dullah make the only logical grouping. All three frequented the North Star Club and hung around with prostitutes, while both Dullah and Miller were fairly serious drug users. All three, too, at least knew both Leanne Vilday and the late Lynette.

The unquestionably odd man out, meanwhile, was Tony Paris. Not only did he not associate with Ronnie, Dullah and Miller, he did not even have John Actie's local notoriety. His one criminal conviction was for shoplifting, something for which he did have something of a reputation. His circle of friends was an old, Afro-Caribbean crowd, based around the Paddle Steamer pub and the Casablanca Club, not the Custom House and the North Star.

It's telling that where the reaction among the local in-crowd to the news of John Actie's arrest was one of weary cynicism, the news of Tony Paris's arrest provoked simple befuddlement. Surely some mistake.

In most of Britain, any assemblage of five black men will be seen as threatening, will be assumed to constitute some kind of gang. Ironically it was only with their convictions and/ or acquittals that a wider public even began to take an interest in what kind of men these might be. The shock of seeing men convicted as murderers and sentenced to life imprisonment propelled some of us, at last, to try to see them as individuals, to wonder what real lives lay behind the familiar stereotypes bandied about by the prosecution and lazily accepted by the press.

First time I heard Stephen Miller's name he was already in prison awaiting trial for the murder of his girlfriend. By the time I met him he was in Wormwood Scrubs doing life for that killing. By then, I really didn't know what to expect. For a start there were the two basic images that emerged from the trial. First, that peddled by the prosecution: Miller the cocaine-addicted pimp who'd worked his girlfriend pitilessly. Second, that proffered by the defence; Miller the hapless man with the mental age of a child and intense vulnerability in the face of the brutal interrogation he underwent at the hands of the police. And what made it more confusing was that both these images seemed to have some grounding in reality.

When I talked to the people who knew him, almost nothing seemed to emerge. Jackie Harris, Dullah's girlfriend, said he used to confide his dreams and ambitions to her but she was unable to say what they might have been. Pepsi Orton was probably the closest friend Miller had in Cardiff, seeing him almost daily in the months before the murder, yet all Pepsi could manage by way of a description was, 'He was all right, easy to get on with. He might have been a pimp but I never saw him beat her or anything.' And that was about all anyone had to offer. Quiet, they said, a loner. And no, no one suspected that his intelligence was so limited; he was certainly streetwise enough.

It was only women who seemed to see through Miller's front. To Leila Attfield of Huttons solicitors he seemed like a big kid, happy watching the cartoons on telly in the prison, and a surprisingly pleasant kid too, certainly by contrast with his co-defendants. 'He was the only one had any manners,' said Attfield. 'I'd go out and buy them fish and chips or whatever and he was the only one who would say "Thanks, Leila". With the rest of them it was just, "Where's the fucking vinegar?" However, Debbie Paul's distinctly unflattering assessment of Miller's resemblance to the 'evil pimp' of the media coverage went like this: 'He could only just about handle Lynette, let alone anyone else. He was so ugly, he was a really ugly man for a black guy.'

But while others too have mentioned that Miller might have changed his clothes more often while he was living in Cardiff, the Stephen Miller I finally met up with in the visitors' room at the Scrubs is a smartly turned-out individual, sporting a crisp blue and white pinstripe shirt and natty gold chain. But it's true that he looks his best from a distance. Take a photo of him and he'd come across as a cool, slick individual. Up close the impression is undermined by his pitted complexion and the hurt and fear in his eyes. As we talk it becomes clear that the hurt is more to do with the reason he's in prison than the experience of prison itself. The institutional life is one he's known since childhood.

'I was in a children's home, watching my mum and dad fight over custody. I love my mum a lot, you know, she's my everything, but . . . I've had a hard life,' he said. Stephen Miller left school at sixteen, went out with a girl called Bernadette who had a baby, Ricky, when he was eighteen. They broke up – Miller doesn't even remember her surname. Not long after he came down to Cardiff to visit his brother Tony, who was living with Francine Cordle. Through Francine, Stephen met Lynette. They started going out together, Stephen coming down regularly until Lynette found the room in Dorset Street, Grangetown, and asked him to come live with her.

'It was just a basic life. We'd watch videos, horror, blue movies, she was into romances. I love my films. We'd watch the news a lot . . . Music, she was into Whitney Houston, Freddie MacGregor. I was into my soul, my Motown. She would go to the North Star, that was her place, the Casablanca was my place. When I did go to the North Star I'd talk to Eugene, or to Ferron . . .'

Looking at the relationship now and from the outside, it seems obvious that here were two people trying to make the best of damaged childhoods. When I put that to Miller, he at first resisted the idea that Lynette had much trouble in her life. He said, 'She was bubbly, she liked to laugh. There may have been bad things in her life but she didn't tell me about them.' But then he conceded, 'She was a secretive person. She had it rough. She went on the game when she was fifteen. And at first I think the money seemed so easy. It's like heroin, she got addicted to it. She was sad because her dad wouldn't let her see her sister. All she wanted was a family and a house.'

So how did he feel about her line of work? 'When I met Lynette she was already on the game. In my heart I wanted her to come off. But I was used to the money, I needed the coke.'

And there you have it. Lynette needed Stephen, wanted someone to live with her and love her, as he did in his way love her. She needed him enough effectively to give up the money she made, to give it all to him. And he needed her, but in the end he needed her for money for drugs. But just to call him a drug addict is to simplify and misunderstand what was going on. Cocaine anyway is not generally recognized as a physically addictive drug, though it is psychologically addictive and Miller had a psyche susceptible to dependency. It would be nice to say that what he needed was love. But for the boy from the children's home, love was maybe not something to be trusted, and what cocaine offered was something better – escape. As he puts it himself, 'At the time I was enjoying myself . . . I was off in my own little fantasy.'

Miller didn't use cocaine like most people – to go out, have a good time interacting with other people – but rather he'd sit alone in his car outside the pub, nursing one or two drinks over the whole evening, listening to his music, smoking his cocaine and dreaming his dreams. But while Stephen was living his fantasy life things were deteriorating. He needed more and more cocaine to keep himself numb and free. Lynette had to work harder and harder to make the money he needed. The street prostitute is locked into a cycle of diminishing returns: when you're young and fresh all the punters want a piece of you but as you become a veteran, and Lynette at twenty was already a veteran, so the demand slackens. Desperation was beginning to creep in on her part. Her colleagues grew pissed off as she'd try to steal their punters, and worried about her as her clothes got shabbier and they heard that she was cutting her prices, offering sex without a condom, as what remained of her self-respect slipped away.

Meanwhile Stephen seemed to be drifting away from her. He rarely wanted to have sex with her anymore, she told Debbie Paul: 'He changed towards her.'

Most observers reckoned that things came to head a week before Lynette died, with the nasty public row in the North Star. Miller, however, downplays its significance: 'We'd had a stupid row. She accused me of sleeping with Maria Veysey. But last time I saw her things were OK: she jumped out of the car with a tin of Breaker in her hand, said she'd see me later.'

But, of course she didn't show. At first he didn't worry too much, she'd run off to one of her aunties before and he preferred to put the blame on the pressure of the Francine Cordle trial hanging over her head.

And so he roamed around Lynette's usual haunts without success, sure that one of her fellow prostitutes must be hiding her. And then, when she was found his dream world shattered and left him at last with regret: 'I know Lynette's up there and she's keeping me strong. We had a love affair. Even though she was a prostitute, she was still a human being. I just wish I'd come off the coke. We could have got out . . .'

They come to my house about half past seven. Tommy Page, he's a bastard, he is, he's nicked me before. Three of them with Tommy Page in charge. I looked out my bedroom window, my wife went down first, then I went down. I said, 'What do you want?' They said, 'We want you to come to the police station.' I said, 'What for?' They said, 'For the murder of Lynette White.' I said, 'Are you fuckin' crazy or what? Fuck off.'

They said 'The chief said we got to bring you in.' I said, 'I'm not fuckin' coming. If you wants me you'll have to fuckin' take me.' He said, 'C'mon, John, we don't want to call back-up and take you in.' I said, 'Go on, call back-up.' I had them on the door for about twenty minutes, they wouldn't run from the house because I had my fucking dog, you know what I mean. And I'm fucking glad I had my fucking dog. I didn't want them police stampeding through my house, my kids were in bed, my daughter was nine months old in a cot. Tommy said, 'Look, John, you'll have to go.' I said, 'Well, come on then . . .' Tommy said, 'No, you'll set the dog on me.' I said, 'Well, I got him for you, as a matter of fact, Tommy, any time you fuckers come to my house.' He said, 'Come on, John, let's not be . . .' I said, 'All right then, go and sit in your car. I'll be out.'

So I went and had a wash and kisses my missus. I phoned my brother, told him the police had come, told him to get in touch with my solicitor. Then I went out, got into the police car, and said, 'You fucking stupid cunts, you're fucking idiots, you are.' We went in the police station, Page took a statement. They left me there for an hour and then the next thing they kicked the door open and about eight of them came in: Dick Powell, fucking Tommy Page, Jock Mitchell . . . Dick Powell says, 'John Arthur Actie, I am now arresting you on suspicion of murdering Lynette White.' Then they put me in a car, took me to fucking Caerphilly. So they put me in a cell up there. I said, 'You stupid fucking bastards,' and went to sleep. The stupid saga started there.

When they arrested him John Actie kept his mouth shut. He'd been in police stations before and he's been in them since, and he reckons he knows the score. For John Actie dealing with the police has less to do with law and order than out-and-out war. John's policy on being captured is to give out name, rank and serial number and leave it at that. Let the police make a case or not. And it's with a soldier's disdain for civilians that he talks about the people who cooperated with the police, Miller and Psaila and Vilday.

'Some people are so weak for the police, you know, you chuck them in a cell for two days, take their clothes off them, they're junkies, they'll do anything. They're just weak people. I didn't know these people till I saw them in court. I don't hang around with prostitutes, I don't even go to their pubs, you know.'

John Actie continues to have an unhappy relationship with the police. Since his acquittal, 'The police have me on four charges already. I went to court the other week, I said, "What's this for now?" They said I have sworn at a policeman on Bute Road. I said, "When, who, which policeman?" They said, "Do you want to plead guilty to obstruction?" I said, "No. I'll contest it." When I goes into court for them little cases I'll do it myself. I won't trouble my solicitor, I'm not stupid, I knows the law. I just sat through the longest trial in British history, if you can't pick up things there . . .'

There is of course a history to all this. John Actie knows that the police haven't just picked his name out of a hat: 'I wasn't no angel. I was running a blues [up to October '87]. I wasn't making a great deal, people used to have a nice time, you know, look forward to a blues. I was working at the Casa most weekends. Sometimes I'd work in Newport, generally around. I'd always get some work. I'd buy and sell things too, you know what I mean, and make some money there.'

As far as the Cardiff police are concerned this account doesn't tell the half of it. Or at least the remark about buying and selling things doesn't. Around 1988 the Docks police figured John Actie for Butetown's heaviest cocaine dealer, a Yardie-connected drug baron.

Talking to people more or less in the know, John Actie was not the Mr Big that the police made him out to be. Yes, he was a drug dealer but not on a grand scale. But he did have a reputation, an image, and that image was largely of his own making. Basically John Actie was the baddest m-f in the neighbourhood. Stories abound of John Actie sorting people out, generally putting the fear of God into anyone standing in his way, failing to pay what they owed, or whatever. This ensured that few people would try to do him down in a business deal and was enough to ensure the respect of a younger generation of kids who fancied themselves as bad men. But it didn't and doesn't make him an Al Capone or a John Gotti.

But then all the indicators are that such a person doesn't exist. Or at least that the people who are making really serious money out of the cocaine trade are not living in Butetown. What Butetown provides is the lower level workforce of the drug industry – medium, small-scale and street-level distributors and dealers.

John Actie loves children and they love him. They clamber all over him like he's a big teddy, this bullet-headed six-foot-something guy, built like the proverbial brick shithouse. If a man laid a hand on John Actie he'd break their arm. John Actie loves children and dogs but he doesn't give a toss for 99·9 per cent of his fellow grown-ups.

The Actie family is huge, one of Cardiff's oldest and largest black families, spread over the Docks, Gabalfa, Mynachdy, Llanrumney. 'My family originate from the Docks. My father was born here, his family's from St Lucia originally. My dad was a seaman, his father was a seaman too, then my dad became a steel erector, worked at Llanwern steelworks, built the Severn Bridge. In the sixties we moved to Llanrumney, me and my dad and my mum and my brothers and sisters.'

It was while living in Llanrumney that John Actie's world collapsed: 'My dad died when I was twelve. He was only forty-two when he died. He was a good man, you know, the best. We were so close. He used to take me to rugby. I used to play rugby for Cardiff Youth. I was flanker or number eight, I used to run for Cardiff Athletics, I played baseball for them as well [Cardiff and Liverpool, the old ports, have had flourishing baseball leagues for decades]. I wanted to become a professional sportsman . . . When he died things went off the rails, I started getting into trouble. It wasn't long before I started going to approved schools.'

The bad boy won the day from the sportsman. In his late teens John Actie graduated to a serious jail term and when he came out it was too late to turn back: 'I came out of jail when I was twenty, after a three-year sentence, and I started drifting into the ganja life, you know, the late nights, the blues,

I started drifting away from sports. That's what's happened, and the years have gone by. I'm thirty now.

'I know I was a bad boy, I was a terrible boy, but I had a good upbringing. My mum, my mum has stuck with me through thick and thin.' John raised his voice: 'She loves me, you know.' Then he lowered it again, 'And I loves her too.'

Writing about John Actie it's tempting to take the easy route, to talk about the bully and villain, the man born to be a doorman and debt collector, or to take the bleeding-heart route and write about the scared little boy who lost his dad and has spent the rest of his life striking out blindly at the world. Trouble with either of these approaches is that it is easy to lose the man who is both these things and inevitably more. What you might say about John Actie, though, is that in this case the owner really does resemble the dog.

John Actie's main reaction when they arrested him was outrage. Outrage firstly at being connected with that kind of crime: 'That crime there, I've seen the pictures, oh God, it was horrendous, terrible. And I've got kids, and if anything else like that happens down here it's going to be down to the person who killed that girl. If I knew anything I would have shopped them the same day. Like I said, I'm no angel, but I don't go round beating up women, or fucking chopping up women. It's just horrific and whoever did that, they deserve to be punished. I mean they don't come out of jail for the rest of their life.'

And outrage second at being associated with a bunch of guys he basically regarded as lowlifes: 'I knew them, they're from the area. But I'd never even drink with them. Me and Ronnie have got nothing in common other than our names. We're on a different circle altogether. It's like he lives in Australia and I lives in fucking Britain. Same with Dullah. Me and Dullah didn't like each other at all, we wouldn't give each other the fucking time of day. Miller, he was a pimp, I didn't hang around with him.'

But though Big John stayed hard as nails on the outside,

he's ready to admit that being charged with murder was still an utterly harrowing experience: 'The day they charged me was like my dad had just died all over again. I couldn't believe it. They was all laughing at me the old bill.

'It was very frightening. I'd only seen it on the TV, read about it in books, but now it's happened to me.' It's still incredible to him, though, that he spent two years in prison when the police case against him seemed to him to be completely ludicrous. He says, 'One time I was there and they came in and says "You was there and Tony Paris ran in with a knife and stabbed her." I said, "Who?!" They said, "Tony Paris." I said, "Oh fucking hell." I was laughing at the interview. I said "You've got Tony Paris stabbing Lynette White? Tony Paris is a shoplifter." I said to my solicitor, "Stuart, tell them to fuck off, I'm going back to my cell, this is crazy."

When the day of sentencing finally arrived he just did not know what to expect. 'I wasn't surprised,' he said, 'I was shocked. I knew in my heart I had to come home, I ain't done nothing. But in my head I knew I was going to jail because it was like that. But when they found the two guilty, then they acquitted my cousin, I still had to wait, you know.

'No one can experience that unless they go through it. It was magnificent. I was standing on the stairs with Dullah, loads of screws, you can imagine, they called him up and said, "Guilty." So I thought "Fucking hell," you know. Then they called me up. A screw had to help me up the stairs, I walked in holding on to the rail. I was close to collapse and the judge said, "How do you find John Arthur Actie?" One or two of the girls was crying and then they said, "Not guilty" and it was like going under an anaesthetic. It was repeating in my head . . . not guilty, not guilty. It was brilliant.

'I was sad, you know, because the other three was convicted. But at the end of the day I was home and that was what I was really concerned about. There was nothing I could do for them by being in there too. All I know is I would be dead by now, because I knows the screws would have killed me, because there's no way that I'm being in jail for a crime I haven't committed without rebelling against the system. So therefore I would have been shipped round every jail in the country and my family would have lost track of me, though my family would go to the end of the world for me, my family is very close, very close. Nothing comes between us.'

None of the accused really believed that their acquittal meant the end of their involvement with the police, but for the others it meant a respite at least. For John, though, it was just one more battle in a war being waged on an almost daily basis. 'I hate this area because of the police. If I go to town and I sees the police my heart goes a hundred miles an hour. Ask my wife, I don't like to go to town now, I won't go to town shopping with my wife. I don't like being up around them. At the same time I won't let them take advantage, and that's what gets me into trouble, I suppose. But why should I have to take shit off them. I just don't know. I sits down and thinks about it. I'm on medication from the doctor, you know, sometimes I can't go out of my house. It's terrible. I've just done two years for a crime I didn't commit . . .'

Yet it's a struggle he feels locked in. There's little question of getting out. Instead he's still scuffling around the margins of the law. 'What I used to do, I used to work on doors. And I used to get work debt collecting. I does some now, you know. I've got to back off it now because of the police. I haven't got a licence so people can easily say, "Oh, he came and threatened me," and that's demanding money with menaces. So what I'll do, I'll get the work and turn it round to someone who's got a licence, and I'll get a percentage.'

And domestically too John knows that this is where he's made his stand and he's resigned to taking what comes. 'I don't bother with many people, apart from a, like, chosen few I will talk to. Don't get me wrong, I'll talk to everyone, all the kids . . . but I feel I'd love to get out of here. But I've got two kids, two girls, it's not that easy.'

Ronnie Actie was thirty when he was arrested for the murder of Lynette White. He was born in the Docks into a large extended family that ran to his having eleven brothers, sisters and half-brothers and sisters. His parents left the Docks when the redevelopment came in the sixties, moved to Splott first and then to Gabalfa, where Ronnie grew up. By the time of the murder he was a known petty criminal, he'd done time for robbery and had a reputation for extorting money out of prostitutes. At that time he hung out mostly in Gabalfa. Sometimes, when they'd finished with Raja's snooker club in Riverside, they'd visit the Docks, though hanging out with some non-Docks white guys made Ronnie just a little bit of an outsider. Late at night, though, Ronnie used to frequent the North Star and it was there that he met Leanne Vilday and inadvertently involved himself in the whole bad business.

Ronnie doesn't like to talk about what happened. Or rather Ronnie would love to talk about what happened, but he'd like to talk about it tomorrow. Or if you can't make that, how about yesterday? It's just that today is always difficult. This is understandable, of course. You go through what he went through and you don't necessarily want to relive it. There were those involved in the campaign, though, who felt that maybe he owed it to the guys inside to make that effort. But still.

Perhaps why Ronnie's attitude seems particularly odd is, when he was in the police station, Ronnie probably talked more than anyone, apart from Miller. It wasn't that Ronnie was weak like Miller either. He just seems to have been baffled. He has a conspiratorial turn of mind and, from his statements to the police, he obviously felt that there must be a reason for his being there, that someone must have set him up somehow. After Miller he was the most closely involved with the dead girl. He was going out with Leanne at the time of the murder. He saw her on the night itself, and now she was testifying against him, saying he was there. Throughout the police interviews, then, there's a sense that the police were not just trying to get information out of Ronnie Actie, but that he was trying to get information out of them. Take, for instance, this exchange, from one of the last interviews before he was formally charged:

DC HAINES: What do you think the reason is that she was
 mutilated?
RONALD ACTIE: . . . it could be money, it could be drugs,
 it could be anything.
DC HAINES: It is either drugs or prostitution and the money
 she was giving . . .
RONALD ACTIE: Or, or somebody else she might have . . .
DC HAINES: . . . the pimps . . .
RONALD ACTIE: she might have ripped somebody off, or
 spoiled a deal . . .

And so it goes on, Ronnie wondering which of his co-accused
might have been capable of the murder – Dullah, maybe, or
Miller whose brother had the bad reputation. And the police
all the while trying to railroad Ronnie into going along with
their ever-changing agenda and ever-changing roster of suspects, culminating in an absolutely ludicrous exchange about
a guy called Michael Taylor's hair and how kinky it might
be. Taylor was an associate of Dullah, with a black father and
a white mother, like Ronnie, but Detective Constables Tooby
and Haines were determined to persuade Ronnie that Taylor
is in fact kind of Greek-looking, in a transparent and fruitless
attempt to rope Taylor in to make sense of Miller's ramblings
in his confession about the two Greek guys on the stairs.

Yet buried in all the rambling and the tail-chasing, Ronnie
does provide some useful information, the police just didn't
seem interested in hearing it. What Ronnie offered was a
description of the way Leanne Vilday was on the night of the
murder:

She came in about five, ten minutes before the club was finishing. Everyone was leaving so she said, 'Oh, take me up to the
Cabbies Club.' I said, 'No, if I takes you up there now, people
are going to see the state of your face, they're automatically
going to think I done it. I'm going down my sister's, do you
want to come down?' So she could wash and clean up her face
and all that. So that's where we went, to my sister Michelle's,

in Angelina Street. My sister was in bed but she came down. She saw Leanne. I remember making some joke like, 'Looks like she's been ten rounds with Marvin Hagler.' She laughed and went back to bed.

Me and Leanne was laying on the settee in my sister's front room. Kissing and cuddling, talking and she wasn't the same. She seemed jumpy. I thought she's just taken a beating off a punter, that's why. So, anyway, I got up to take my jumper off and she said to me, 'Oh Lynette, Lynette has been missing for a few days.' So I said, 'Oh.' I wasn't taking much notice. So she said, 'Oh, she could have been murdered or something.' I started laughing and said, 'Don't be stupid, she can look after herself.'

Anyway I took my jumper off and that, laid down on the settee kissing and cuddling. I dropped off. So she woke me up about six in the morning. She said to me, 'Oh, Ronnie, I'm going.' So I said, 'Oh, all right then.' 'Cause I'd only had a little bit of sleep, she just woke me up and I didn't feel like giving her a lift anyway, but thinking about it now I should have given her a lift. And off she went. I thought afterwards she was brave for walking down on her own because it was still dark.

This statement clearly implies that Leanne already knew at least something of what had happened to Lynette, and had, more than likely, already seen the body. And that Ronnie had nothing to do with it but was rather the person she ran to for a little human comfort after an appalling shock.

But the police weren't interested in following that line of thinking and Ronnie himself, when it came to the trial, kept his mouth shut and didn't come to the witness stand, as he reckoned that whatever good he might have done his cause would have been firmly undone if the prosecution had been able to bring in a criminal record that included the attempted robbery of a prostitute, at knife point. And, as things worked out, who's to say he was wrong?

Tony Paris is not much more than five feet tall, wears thick glasses, sports a serious Cardiff accent and wore his hair short and natural before his arrest, but had it cropped in prison. On release he added a Malcolm X goatee – and an outsize personality.

First time I met Tony Paris was in Wormwood Scrubs and before he made it across the visitors' room to the table where I was sitting he'd already stopped to banter with all the prison guards and half the prisoners. Prison was not going to get Tony Paris down, he was hell bent on joking it into submission. It soon became apparent was that this chirpiness was his shield, that here was a fiercely proud man who was simply not going to let prison drag him down. Beneath the surface bounce, Tony Paris is in many ways the toughest of the defendants and his bonhomie is largely directed at getting what he wants.

On 10 December 1988 Tony Paris was thirty years old, married to Denise, father of a three-year-old boy, a professional shoplifter and nightclub doorman. When he was arrested on suspicion of murder that morning, his first question was 'who's been murdered then?' When they told him it was the Lynette White killing he couldn't believe it, said, 'Fine, let's go down to the station and sort this out. Someone's got this well bollocksed.'

And if Tony couldn't believe he was being charged with murder nor could anyone else in Butetown. Tony knew everybody, what with having been born and bred in the Docks, and working the clubs. Tony Paris stood out from the pack: some might believe that any of the others might be guilty of such a crime – John's reputation has long gone beyond his actual deeds, Yusef and Ronnie were both hard men with a known capacity for violence and Miller was after all the girl's boyfriend, and a serious cocaine user. But Tony, Tony Paris? Nah, no way.

Tony Paris was born in Butetown in 1957, the third of seven children but the first to be born in Wales. Tony's parents had come over from Nevis and his father was working on the Docks. They lived in Butetown from the first and stayed there, in Hodges Square, when the redevelopment came. Tony went to school at St Mary's first, where he was an altar boy, and then to Fitzalan High School. For a lot of Butetown kids leaving the Docks to go to Fitzalan led to an abrupt realization that skin colour might not be the big issue in Butetown, but it sure as hell was in the big bad outside world.

Tony didn't experience it like that, though. For him it was more a question of teenagers forming into gangs: he was part of the Docks gang, then you had your Grangetown gang, your Canton gang and so on. Whatever, he left school the summer of his fifteenth birthday and got a job with an engineering firm, worked there six years, got a couple more similar jobs over the next three, four years and then it was 1982 and the recession closed South Wales down. Tony stayed in Butetown, worked the clubs and drifted into serious shoplifting. He was caught once, in 1986, and the resultant publicity – 'Rastafarian caught shoplifting' said the headline in the local paper – didn't cause him to give up shoplifting but it did lead to him cutting off his dreadlocks, livid at the imputation that Ras Tafari might somehow be to blame for his crimes.

Tony became a regular Butetown Fagin or, as he likes to put it, 'a black Santa Claus'. If you needed a new outfit for the kids, Tony was your man. Meanwhile he kept on working the clubs, meeting and greeting the people on the door, any excuse to dress up in the old tuxedo and chat up all the ladies on their way in. The Casa was his regular gig, as his mate Peter Scott was managing the place, and that was where his contemporaries – Sinclair, Saleh, Sweeney and the rest – liked to hang out, listening to the sound systems, smoking and shooting some pool.

Tony, however, knew all the women involved in the murder. Lynette he knew from when she was a baby girl, her family being Docks people too and Tony's father drinking with Terry White even. Some people, Miller among them, reckoned Tony might have been interested in pimping Lynette at one time. Tony denies it, says Miller was just jealous of anyone talking to his woman.

Leanne was Tony's little brother Paulie's baby's mother.

And while the rest of the Paris clan didn't know or didn't want to know, and Paulie himself was obliged to keep clear, Tony was happy to be little Craig's uncle and would often bring Leanne gifts for the baby.

Tony even knew Angela Psaila. Went to bed with her once even. Something he's less than proud of. 'She was a monster,' he says, 'but sometimes it's a case of any port in a storm, you know what I mean.' For Tony the most embarrassing moment of the trial was the point when the barrister asked him if he had ever slept with Angela Psaila. He was desperate to deny it but couldn't be sure what she might say or what would happen if he was caught lying. So he admitted it. And to his eternal chagrin she denied it.

It was this dalliance with Angela Psaila that, in my view, dragged Tony Paris into this mess. None of the other original witnesses ever named him. Grommek, Atkins, Vilday and Violet Perriam never mentioned him, but Angela Psaila, at the end of her long rambling statement of 17 December, after naming John Actie, Ronnie Actie, Stephen Miller, Tony Miller, Dullah, Tony Brace and Jack Ellis, has a sudden after-thought: 'Oh, and Tony Paris came by selling ganja.'

Even then no one was too bothered. Tony Brace and Jack Ellis were soon enough dropped from the investigation but still Tony's name was there, and it was one of those that the police ran by Stephen Miller. And to Miller it was a kind of lifeline, a name he wasn't frightened of, that he could lay all this off on. Even Paris himself surmises Miller may have picked his name out deliberately, precisely because it was so absurd. Thus preparing the way for him, 'to turn round later and say to the police: How could you accept a confession like that? It's absurd, for God's sake. I've made Tony Paris the murderer. Surely you can see that's a joke.' If it was a joke though it was one that it'll take Tony a while to see the funny side of.

He went into the police station that morning expecting to be out in a matter of moments and emerged four years later.

*   *   *

124

Yusef Abdullahi they sent to another prison. I drove up with Malik on a cold spring morning to Gartree, tucked away in the middle of nowhere between Leicester and Market Harborough. Talking to Yusef over several cups of tea, cans of Coke, and packets of custard creams and bourbon biscuits, in the strikingly 1960s British Rail catering environment characteristic of prison visiting rooms, it rapidly became clear that this is a rather different scene to the Scrubs.

Where Tony was busy ducking and diving, making the prison work for him, Yusef seemed to have found a certain seriousness in Gartree. As fate would have it, Yusef happened to be inside with Winston Silcott, the man falsely convicted of the killing of PC Blakelock, and Raphael Rowe, jailed for the M25 murder but also protesting his innocence. These three had evidently got a black-consciousness-raising thing going on – as betokened by Yusef's current fondness for billing himself as Yusef X.

Yusef is possessed of a powerful rage, not just at his plight but also at those he sees as responsible. Those Yusef deems responsible include the racists who run this society and the police who patrol Butetown. Yet it's a politicized rage, far more directed at the system in general than its particular agents. Thus he's keener to talk about the racism of British justice than the perfidy of, for instance, his common-law wife Jackie, or the more-or-less friends like Ronnie Williams and Leanne Vilday, who testified against him.

A happy infancy in Butetown was rudely interrupted by a forced move when Yusef was eight and Butetown was in the process of being rebuilt. Out in the depressed white working-class suburb of Ely he discovered racism. His father would be abused on the way home from work, his mother Pauline, a white woman, would have to put up with a gamut of vileness when she took her kids to the nursery.

A bad time touched bottom when Yusef's father died during the Ely sojourn. He suffered a heart attack at home, and Pauline went down the street banging on doors asking to use a telephone to call for an ambulance. No one would help and she had to keep on going till she eventually found a phone box. The ambulance arrived too late to be of use.

If there was an upside to this awfulness it was that the Abdullahis then left Ely. The Somali community in Butetown was still a tightly knit one at this time, and one well capable of looking after its own, as Yusef remembers, 'The community was staunch back then, if a father died then the next in line took over.' So the Abdullahis were taken in by relatives.

Yusef went back to school in Butetown to be taught, like several generations of kids, by the redoubtable Mrs Betty Campbell. But when it came to be time to go to secondary school, Yusef was just in time to be part of a social experiment. There's no secondary school in Butetown itself, so previously almost all the Butetown children had gone to Fitzalan High School. The new policy, however, decided that, in the interests of greater harmony, the Butetown kids should be dispersed throughout the city's schools. On the ground this didn't necessarily seem like such a great idea. Certainly it didn't work for Yusef. As he tells it he was constantly in trouble, would miss school and show up at Fitzalan instead, to be with his friends, was beaten up by a teacher, sent to the police station by another teacher when he was barely fourteen, and finally expelled.

The Somali community had a policy of shipping unruly teenagers back to Africa, to teach them some respect for the real business and hardship of life. Yusef was slated to go, but instead he ran off to Epsom with a yen to become a jockey. His apprenticeship to the horse game seemed to have set him on the straight and narrow, but after a year or so a couple of pub fights landed Yusef in prison and out of a racing berth.

Out of prison and the die was firmly cast. The next decade coasted by, odd straight jobs in the pubs and clubs supplemented a hustler's life. 'I was just a man who worked the clubs,' says Yusef, 'I'd sell speed, cannabis . . .'

Yusef put his dreams aside and got on with being a bad man. How bad a man, though, it's hard to know. Yusef of course plays down that side of his character, but a more complex picture emerges from talking to the woman who Yusef was at his baddest towards – his common-law wife Jackie Harris, the woman whose testimony helped to convict him.

At the time of the arrest Jackie had taken an injunction out against Dullah to keep him away from her and the kids on account of his violence. After the arrest, the police did everything in their power to persuade her to testify. In their favour was the fact that she was close to a policeman, Jeff Smith, who had helped her with getting the injunction. Also they knew Jackie liked to be in the midst of a drama.

Shortly before Dullah's arrest Jackie's potential as a drama queen was demonstrated by the strange business of the 'kidnap' case. As told by Malik and Alex – not the most impartial of witnesses but not ones automatically to take Dullah's part either – Jackie had left their daughter with a neighbour, Dullah had come round unexpectedly and taken her off with him. And next thing he knew Jackie was on the local news sobbing and claiming that her child had been kidnapped by the father who was going to take her off to Somalia. This was news to Dullah who brought the kid back only to discover that the terminally distraught Jackie had taken the opportunity to spend a night out down the pub.

So the police reckoned that Jackie Harris had potential: she was separated from and in the midst of an almighty battle with Dullah, and she didn't have any hang-ups about talking to the police. Jackie told them that Dullah had threatened that if she didn't behave she'd end up like that Lynette White, charming things like that. It fell short of a confession, but still backed up the prosecution's case nicely. Come the trial, Jackie exploited its dramatic potential for all it was worth: tears, retractions, endless changes of mind as to whether she would testify or not – all variations on a theme of 'he's bad to the bone but I loves him'.

After she testified and Dullah was found guilty, Jackie didn't want to go back to living in the Docks. She intimated that she might be in danger if she did, so the police and social services found her a place outside Cardiff.

Up in the Valleys, past Caerphilly, up and over the side of the valley, on a grim, grey little estate, Jackie's flat is as near to the middle of nowhere as makes no difference. She is sitting in the kitchen with a bunch of other women from the area, drinking cups of tea and smoking a spliff – dope in the Valleys is less a subcultural thing than an essential aid to beating the boredom, and it seems like practically everyone under forty likes a toke.

Tiffany, Jackie's youngest, is playing in the living room, the older children are at school. Jackie and I sit around the table to talk while Malik sits on the sofa, in front of the TV, leafing through Jackie's old photos. Jackie's a wiry woman with short tousled hair and small, neat features. And she has something – a degree of electricity about her – that makes her the focus of attention. When she talks, her characteristic speedy self-absorption is intermittently lit up by bursts of real warmth.

'I was born in Germany,' she said. 'My father was in the forces. He was from the Docks. My mother came from Barry originally. Then he went to work on the oil rigs, he's a self-made millionaire now in the oil business import/export.' He's also unfortunately no longer with Jackie's mother, and it was with her mum that she remained, moving back to Cardiff, to the Docks where her mum married again, this time to Pete McCarthy, the licensee of the Custom House at the time of the murder.

Jackie left school at sixteen. 'I did lots of different jobs and started a family almost immediately,' she said. 'Had my first daughter when I was seventeen. She died two days later and I had another almost immediately, and the rest have just come by accident, none of them have been planned. My eldest was for a policeman. He's still a policeman in Cardiff, he's a black guy from the Docks. We lived together for a number of years, but our second child had a serious heart complaint and that put a terrible strain on us. She's fine now apart from an occasional bout of pneumonia.'

Suddenly we've plunged deep into chat-show melodrama. Jackie seems to be someone who's always acting in their own private show. For me, she's rehearsing an appearance on 'Kilroy' or 'Oprah' – investigating sexual morality today. 'Jackie,' Oprah will say, 'you're twenty-nine years old and from South Wales. Tell us about your man troubles. Go on, girl.'

'Well, I met Dullah when I worked as a DJ in Mel's club in the Docks. He came to live with me in my house in Grangetown. I've got two kids with him, Joseph and Tiffany, and then I had the snip. No more. I don't think it's right for a lot of kids to be brought up with all different fathers. I think two's the limit so I got sterilized. Because obviously, you know, I'm not always sat at home. I do have a love life!

'Dullah was violent from the start. He'd come in one night and he'd start and it wouldn't stop there with a slap. It would go on for days. I wouldn't be able to go out. It was terrible. We would have crazy times, me as well as him, but there's never a reason to hit someone. I don't know why I stayed with him. Maybe because there was nowhere to go. He was very much in authority. If he said jump I had to jump. I think he regarded me more as a possession than a person in my own right. Dullah thinks that women should be confined to indoors, round the cooker and having babies. I didn't have them views. I left him on a number of occasions, I've taken out injunctions and he's always come back. He'd be back saying I'm sorry and I'd still say no. And he can't take rejection so the hidings would start and then I'd have to take him back so the hidings would stop. I would actually run to my parents but he would always come and drag me back. Until I found Women's Aid.'

Around the time of the murder their relationship was at a low point. 'This is what would happen each day,' said Jackie. 'I'd get up, get a pile of abuse from Dullah, get the children off to school, go round Alex's, come home, do the cleaning, and he'd be lying in bed, or be out at the bookie's. There'd be fifty thousand people coming through the house every day, local boys, drug dealers, everybody.

'Teatime the kids would come home, chaotic. Dullah would play with the kids, he was good with the kids, he'd read them stories and things, then it would be bedtime for the kids and we'd sit down and I'd probably get stoned. Then he'd probably go out to one of the clubs, North Star, Casablanca . . . And then when he got back the trouble would start. He'd accuse me of messing around or something. He'd wake me up with a punch in the head. I have nightmares about that still, then he'd say, "Get up, make me some coffee, make me something to eat", "You done this", slap, "You done that", slap.'

So what went wrong with the relationship? To hear Jackie tell it, practically everything. There was the drugs, the pointlessness of it all and, above all, there was the violence. 'I was demoralized, I felt completely degraded, I didn't feel like a woman I felt like the scum of the earth. I was taking sleeping pills. I'm still a bit headshot. It was an ordeal. He demoralized me physically, sexually, mentally, he took my rights away not just as a woman but as a human being.'

Of course Dullah sees it somewhat differently. He blames their break-up on Jackie having an affair with the policeman, Jeff Smith. It's an accusation that Jackie steadfastly denies. 'Jeff Smith was on vice when I was working at the Custom House and one day Dullah had given me a real hiding,' she said. 'I was just unrecognizable when I walked into work and this copper on vice said, "You've got to get an injunction and this is how you do it." Dullah said Jeff Smith got the injunction himself, but he didn't. He just gave me the advice and that's his duty as a policeman. To give advice.'

Any way you look at it, though, Jackie had had a bad enough time from Dullah for the news of his arrest for Lynette White's murder to provoke distinctly mixed emotions. As she remembered that time we were propelled into another 'Oprah' show: My husband was a killer – Murderers' wives speak out! 'When I heard Dullah had been arrested it was like one big puzzle all fitting into place. Needles, Miller being in the house, Dullah knocking around with Leanne, things that were said . . . it all made sense. So, though I was gutted because he was my kids' father, it really wasn't a big shock. And though I was gutted I was also relieved. My initial thought was I won't have to worry about him breaking my windows and coming in in the middle of the night. We can go home, kids. Then the full horror hit me. I couldn't go home.'

When it came to the trial Jackie repeated those things that were said, the threats she claimed Dullah had made. I asked her whether she really thought remarks about 'not wanting to end up like Lynette' were really half-way admissions or rather just typical of the brutality with which Dullah treated her. 'Well, those were the kinds of things he'd say,' she said. 'He was cruel, he was sick. He said, "You'll be shocked when you find out who it is, it's somebody you know very well." He seemed to know loads about it. I think he was probably just showing off. That was Dullah anyway, he would say something just to freak you out. This time his mouth got him into trouble, because he convinced me, he convinced me enough to go into the box and give evidence against him.

'One part of me wants to believe he wasn't there. The other part says you know the other side of him, get real. He was certainly capable of being there and doing it. But . . . Dullah gave me a lot of severe hidings, but he'd get to a stage and think, "Oh God, what have I done?" A couple of times we did have a fight with a knife, and straight away he'd come to and he'd tend to my wounds. So I don't know . . .

'I feel, if he'd taken part, surely I'd have known. There would have been blood, or something. All right, the way he was jacking up . . . his head was shot. But surely he'd have to have a motive . . . I can't honestly see them all standing there saying, "You've got to have a go, because I did." I mean, they're men, they're men in their own right.'

And then, in apparent contradiction of the foregoing, Jackie switched tack and accused the police of coercing her into testifying: 'I felt extremely pressured. If I'd known that had I married Dullah I wouldn't have to give evidence then I would have taken that drastic step. I went into court on the second trial and the judge threatened me with fourteen days for contempt if I didn't testify. So I was pressurized. I would never have given evidence voluntarily.'

And she finished with this: 'I love him. When he got sentenced I've never felt so heartbroken. I didn't leave him because I didn't love him, I left him because he was violent. And I'll always love him but I'll never go back. I know when he comes out and I find out he's with someone, it's going to kill me.'

So how did three out of these five men come to be convicted? As we've seen, to a Swansea jury the five must have looked pretty much like a dangerous gang. And so somehow the balance of proof had altered. It should have been the case that the burden was on the prosecution to prove that these five men were there, despite the complete lack of forensic evidence to support this allegation. But instead the defence had been left desperately attempting to prove that they were not there, that they had alibis. And that, as we've seen, wasn't easy.

Secondly, it may well be that the police's handling of the case in general and Stephen Miller in particular was insufficiently criticized by the defence.

But thirdly, and most strangely, the defence somehow failed entirely to discredit the evidence of Psaila, Vilday, Grommek and Atkins, an extraordinary ragbag of evident fictions and self-contradictions though it all was. Indeed, it may be that this immense confusion of names and the endless contradictory statements actually worked in favour of the prosecution case. There was such a mass of tangled allegations that a bewildered jury may have ended up feeling that such a lot of smoke could not have been generated without some kind of a fire.

The defence strategy was simply to combat the witnesses in court, to confront them with the evidence of the myriad contradictions in their statements. This, the defence teams justifiably reckoned, should have been enough to discredit these witnesses in the eyes of judge and jury. And, indeed, the judge firmly expressed his doubts as to the value of the key witnesses. But in order to be given a chance of success, this plan had to be underpinned by an explication of the pattern that lay behind these statements, thereby showing just how the puffs of smoke had been orchestrated.

For instance, Leanne Vilday and Mark Grommek, in their initial statements, made remarkably similar allegations. Both named Ronnie Actie, Yusef Abdullahi and Martin Tucker plus an unknown black man with shoulder-length dreadlocks and (maybe) a goatee beard. The one variation in their stories is that Leanne also names Stephen Miller as being there.

Now the police might have argued that the reasons for the initial discrepancies in the witnesses' statements were due to fear or confusion. However, that does not begin to explain why both Vilday and Grommek should have arrived at the same story. After all, of the four men they both referred to, only two were actually tried for the crime. What seems incredible is that they should have simultaneously and independently invented a tall black man with shoulder-length dreadlocks, let alone that they should both have plucked the name of Martin Tucker out of thin air.

Tucker, after all, turned out to be convincingly alibied, upon which discovery Leanne Vilday withdrew his name from her statement, claiming that she had included his name simply out of malice 'because I hate him, that's why'. This might be a plausible explanation – though it hardly instils much faith in Vilday as an honest witness – if it were not the case that Grommek too had named Tucker.

Rather the remarkable similarity between the Vilday and Grommek statements suggests two main possibilities: either their story is the truth or it's a fabrication jointly made up by the pair of them. The first option seems to be contradicted by Tucker's alibi amongst much else, so we must consider the strong possibility that Grommek and Vilday's statements are the results of a collaboration and are both untrue and unreliable. In this respect it is also worth remembering that while at the time of the murder Leanne and Angela were friends and didn't know Grommek, by the time of their arrests Leanne was no longer living with Angela but was friendly with Grommek.

The question that remains is why? Why should Grommek and Vilday make up the particular story they did, implicating those particular people? The answer, initially, lies with Grommek. He was the next link in the chain after the police had succeeded in getting a statement out of Angela Psaila. On 17 November she alleged that one of the two gays had opened the door to Ronnie Actie who had been hanging around outside with a group of other men.

So when the police pulled Grommek in on 22 November it is reasonable to assume that they confronted him with this allegation and suggested that he was the man who answered the door. Grommek eventually admitted to this. Then came the question of who it was that he let in. Psaila had provided the name of Ronnie Actie; the police must have asked who else was with Ronnie.

Now Grommek knew Ronnie only from the North Star Club, where he had recently become the DJ (and also where he had become friendly with Leanne Vilday). Two people Ronnie used to associate with in the North Star were Tucker and Abdullahi. Significantly enough, Ronnie did not tend to see either of them except in the North Star. Furthermore they were recent associates, guys who had not been friends of his at the time of the murder. So what Grommek appears to have done is to have responded to the suggestion that Ronnie Actie had been at his door with a bunch of mates, by naming the people he thought of as Ronnie Actie's mates – Tucker, Dullah and a black man with dreadlocks (perhaps another North Star regular, Derek Ferron).

It is possible that Grommek had already talked to Vilday about what to say before he made this statement and that she may have helped in deciding what names to name. However, seeing as this list includes her then boyfriend Ronnie and her drug dealer Dullah, it seems more likely that it was all Grommek's own work – particularly in view of the fact that while Vilday continually changed her story Grommek stuck pretty much to his original statement, maintaining even in court that Tucker was there.

It then seems probable that, after Grommek was allowed to go by the police, he must have talked to Vilday and told her what he'd said. So, when she was pulled in on 11 December and finally realized that she was going to be staying there until she started to talk, she repeated Grommek's stories. This being the case – and bearing in mind that all Vilday's subsequent statements simply consist of changes made to make this first story coincide with the Angela Psaila tale and the results of the police investigations of the suspects – it once again seems reasonable to suggest that Vilday's and Grommek's statements are collections of lies made by proven liars and as such are less than worthless as evidence.

Angela Psaila's evidence is rather harder to unravel, largely because of its spectacular incoherence. Her first statement puts a whole troupe of characters outside the murder flat: the North Star's doorman Tony Brace, and regular cabdriver Jack Ellis, her flatmate Leanne's boyfriend Ronnie Actie (who had turned Angela down when she made sexual overtures to him), Lynette's boyfriend Stephen Miller, Angela's sometime affair Tony Paris, plus Leanne's and Ronnie's friend Yusef Abdullahi, and finally Butetown's most wanted man, John Actie.

These clearly fail to add up to any kind of a coherent group and Angela herself seems to have realized this; by her account they are simply part of a changing scene out on James Street over the period of several hours. The involvement of Tony Brace, Jack Ellis and Tony Paris is presented as minimal: Ellis is just driving his taxi and Tony Paris allegedly taking the opportunity to sell ganja to the assembled throng – which, if true, would have been a considerable feat of selling coals to Newcastle, given the occupations of several of those present.

Overall this is such a hazy catch-all kind of statement that it can really only be read as a response to extreme police pressure to name names. It is a response made by a woman who generally kept to herself and was not too well acquainted with the Butetown underworld, as became apparent from the fact that most of the accused scarcely knew of her existence. Basically Angela Psaila blurted out the names of practically every man around Butetown that she knew, and hoped that that would satisfy her accusers – while distancing herself as far as possible from the action.

A detail that tends to bear this theory out is her reference to 'Johnnie Actie'. Nobody calls John Actie 'Johnnie'. Angela must either have been humouring them and getting the name wrong or more likely simply getting in a muddle, talking about the Ronnie Actie she did know rather than the John Actie she didn't.

Further statements from Angela Psaila seem, like those made by Vilday, to have been made simply in response to police pressure to iron out the contradictions and impossibilities in the original statements. In the statement she made on 5 December, for instance, Psaila indicated that Tony Paris had miraculously taken over the place in the scheme of things formerly occupied by Tony Brace, who has disappeared along with Jack Ellis and his cab. In fact this statement marks the first appearance of the line-up who were eventually tried for the murder. Psaila, however, further spoiled whatever trust one might have been prepared to invest in her account when, in her next statement, made on 11 December, she started out with the same crew of five but once she had put them all in the murder room she suddenly added Miller's brother Tony into the action.

Paul Atkins is the one prosecution witness whose account of what happened seems roughly feasible. Atkins's initial statement, made on 22 November, said simply that Grommek opened the door to a man, that they then heard a man's voice asking a woman, presumably Lynette, for sex, and her refusing, followed by an awful scream. Some minutes later Atkins went down to investigate. On the stairs he bumped into Leanne Vilday who'd apparently just entered the building. She kicked the door in and they discovered the brutalized body of Lynette.

Leanne then said she'd tell the police and Atkins went back

upstairs. And that was that. Later Atkins's statements have him encountering, either in the room, outside the room or on the stairs either three or four men, amongst them Ronnie Actie and Dullah, plus a short white man and/or the inevitable tall black man with shoulder-length dreadlocks.

Under cross-examination, though, Atkins told defence lawyers that '[the police] made it pretty clear to me that they didn't believe me when I told them I knew nothing about the murder. They told me things they believed had happened that night. They told me some people they suspected were involved . . . one of those persons they named was Ronnie Actie . . . They were threatening me . . . They threatened to charge me with an offence in connection with the murder. I think that was an offence of conspiracy to murder. They told me I would be charged with an offence unless I told them Ronnie Actie and the others were involved.'

If these allegations are true, they are a damning indictment of the way the police prosecuted this case, demonstrating that a kind of tunnel vision had taken them over as they attempted to make a case out of Mark Grommek's rather desperate fantasy. And in so doing, in their determination to believe what Grommek said without acknowledging they'd all but put the words into his mouth, they ignored the rather less sensational evidence provided by Atkins's initial statement.

This statement from Atkins comes as near as anything in this case to making sense. It suggests that one, as yet unknown, man came into 7 James Street, demanded sex from Lynette White and then, for reasons also unknown but presumably pathological, killed her. Her screams were heard by Atkins and Grommek, who waited till the coast appeared to be clear before investigating, rather than blundering into the middle of things. It also suggests that Leanne Vilday simply stumbled upon the murder either because she had been passing and heard the screams, perhaps on her way to the North Star, or because she had just decided – having been, by Atkins's testimony, drinking – to call into what was, after all, her flat, and see if Lynette was there. This would then explain Leanne's odd behaviour with Ronnie Actie that night – suddenly wondering aloud if Lynette had been murdered, and so on – and the somewhat contrived way in which she appeared to find the body the next evening.

Finally, this version would also provide an explanation for the guilty attitudes displayed by all four major prosecution witnesses. But the guilt that binds them together, given this model, is not to do with any actual involvement in the killing but rather in having very little knowledge about it and having, more or less explicitly, conspired to say nothing about it. All four of them, two gays and two prostitutes, were well aware that they were precisely the kind of people that the law tends not to smile upon. So, faced with a bloody murder in their midst, it is easy enough to imagine that all of them were desperate to stay as far away from it as possible.

Yet, paradoxically, it may have been precisely that guilt at having concealed their real, limited, knowledge of the murder, and thus having had to lie repeatedly to the police, that led, ultimately, to this baroque tale of a five-man killing team. The most plausible explanation is that this bunch of liars possessed of a little guilty knowledge held out on a police force that had become desperate for a prestigious solution to the case. And, once the police had discovered these witnesses who had already lied to them about their involvement in the case, they smelt blood and were simply not prepared to listen to evidence that would return the case to square one – a lone sex killer and no leads.

The trial verdict left Butetown doomstruck. The older generation tended more or less to believe it; accept it at least. The younger generation just saw it as one more example of their powerlessness in the face of a corrupt and racist 'system' as exemplified by the Butetown police.

Or rather, most of them saw it that way. Among those who didn't were the Paris and Abdullahi families, particularly Tony's brother Lloyd and sister Rosie and Yusef's brother Malik and sister-in-law Alex. They talked to a couple of sympathetic probation officers who had attended the trial and were convinced that it had been a terrible miscarriage of justice. And so the probation officers drafted a letter for the families to send to the press, outlining their objections to the verdict.

The first place to bite was the black weekly newspaper, *The Voice*. Heenan Bhatti from *The Voice* came down to find out more and provided the families with a vital initial link to the media world. Bhatti's piece led to the black current affairs programme, 'The Black Bag', deciding to make a documentary on the affair of 'The Cardiff Three', as it began to be known. To coincide with the documentary Bhatti co-wrote a piece for the *Observer* with David Rose, and suddenly the campaign had a public profile.

Meanwhile meetings began to be held in Butetown. The first one attracted three hundred people and a committee was set up. Cutting across 'community bodies', this was a genuinely communal effort run by the black sheep and not by the same old faces, forever looking for handouts from the CBDC. 'Community leaders' therefore were somewhat sniffy but the campaign was snowballing without them. People came forward to design posters and write leaflets; unions affiliated to the campaign and the Trotskyite left incorporated it into its list of potentially revolutionary good causes. The politicos were never able to take over the campaign, however. From the start it was a defiantly local, communal affair, typified by the spontaneous march of late summer 1991, led by the women and children.

Which brings me back at last to where I came in.

EIGHT

Butetown Days, Part Two

Into November 1991 now, back on the train, coming down to see the Reverend Al Sharpton. An appearance by the Reverend Al is Malik's latest publicity coup. Sharpton, the elaborately bouffanted black American agitator, has been in Britain before, to lend his support to the Rolan Adams campaign in the south-east London new-town sprawl of Thamesmead – a campaign formed to ensure that the racist thugs responsible for the murder of a black teenager were a) brought to justice and b) identified as the racists they undoubtedly are. Sharpton's over again for a return visit to Thamesmead and, his attention having been drawn to the Butetown business, he's agreed to take part in the march organized for this weekend.

Critics of Sharpton, of whom there are many, accuse him of cynical self-promotion, but the fact remains that he will continue to play a part as long as he lends his support to campaigns, like the Rolan Adams one and like this one, that more reputable, temperate politicians are too scared to commit themselves to.

Disembark at Cardiff Central, catch a cab and soon enough I'm standing on James Street, outside the murder flat, on a beautiful autumn morning, waiting for something to happen. The SWP are here handing out placards, plus a knot of locals, mainly women and children. Alex and the kids are there holding banners, while Malik and Lloyd are off rendezvousing with the Reverend. Nothing much is going on, so I adjourn to Babs's Bistro for a bacon sandwich. Inside the only other customers are a table of policepersons, who seem just as relaxed and hazy as to what's actually going on as everyone else.

Back out on the street, the crowd is starting to thicken, various members of the Actie clan prominent among them. John's there and Ron senior, but no sign of Ronnie. Wait a little longer and the star attraction finally appears. The Reverend Al rolls up in a stretch Mercedes, no less. First out of the car are the bodyguards, six young black men in all-black uniforms and dark glasses. They're impressive enough but clearly more showbiz than anything else – resembling the rap combo Public Enemy's on-stage minders, Security of the First World, rather than the kind of hard-eyed hombres who surround a Bill Clinton or a John Major in public.

Next out of the car is the Reverend Al, and he is something to behold. From amongst the crowd there's a startled female cry of 'Barry White'. For the Reverend Al is clearly showbiz too, and does indeed bear a remarkable resemblance to the sultan of sex'n'soul, King Barry 'I'm Gonna Love You Just A Little Bit More' White, particularly in the preternatural luxuriousness of his mane, and the baby-pimp softness of his complexion. The photographers crowd around, the police hustle us into a column, and the march is under way.

The march moves down Bute Street all the way to the bottom, turns right at the Ice Rink, and snakes around the prison before heading through the pedestrian shopping precinct of Queen Street and ending up on the steps of the Law Courts. Word comes back that the Reverend Al is not entirely pleased at the length of the stroll, but still, it's a good-humoured affair, the crowd has swollen considerably and the response from passers-by seems positive.

Next up are the speeches – Malik first, then a woman from the SWP, a man from the Black Caucus, Rolan Adams's father, and finally the main event, Al Sharpton. The earlier speakers suffer from the growing sense of expectation: Malik lays out the essential facts well enough, but the SWP speaker goes on somewhat in her efforts to provide a Trotskyist perspective on the case. Then the Black Caucus guy heats things up with some black nationalist rhetoric, firmly stating that this case is at root a matter of racism. Mr Adams is direct, moving and angry; he too sees racism as the key to what's happening here, and little wonder. The stage, then, is set for something truly inflammatory from the Rev.

But no, Sharpton turns out to be the soul of moderation. He eschews the race card, instead points out the reality of the situation, that this is a mixed black and white crowd, representing a mixed community, and that the way to justice is essentially for black and white to unite and fight. It's all delivered with a panache learned in the church and honed on the streets of New York, and all in all is something of a model of radical public speaking, marred only by the fact that he appeared to believe himself to be in somewhere called 'Candiff'. But still . . .

After the rally there's a crush of reporters trying to talk to Sharpton, so I head over to Malik who is talking to his sister, Yasmin, and his mum, Pauline. Introductions are made and Malik tells me that there's an all-day fund-raising party back at the Big Windsor. So I take a walk, through the Saturday shoppers down from the Valleys, past the buskers and the football fans, through the relative calm of Butetown and on to the Docks.

Soon enough I'm sat round a table with Keith Morell, Pepsi, Lloyd and all. They're smoking and drinking and kicking back, with a tangible sense now that things are starting to move, that the campaign is achieving a life of its own. Sat opposite us are Rolan Adams's parents, soft drinks in front of them, talking to the Black Caucus guy. Watching Richard Adams talk, he strikes me as immensely dignified and possessed of something that is beyond bitterness.

And seeing him puts me in mind of a friend I once had, a black woman who was my age, maybe twenty-two then, and she had a little brother who was maybe ten years old. And he died. There was a fire, he was lighting a fire and it went wrong and the ointment that he put on his chest because he had asthma, which asthma he partly had because he was almost the only black kid in the nice white school his mum had sent him to and that situation helped to make him a nervous child, that ointment caught fire. And he died the next day, twelve or eighteen hours later. And after that things were different. For a while we were close, closer even. I had been with her when she heard and in some way I was a part of what happened, but things were different. And after a while, once what had happened became *what had happened*, it became clear that maybe what was worst about what had happened was that *in some way it was not unexpected*. At some level that is what being black in a racist society means: that one can be sure of nothing, not even that one will not be killed. That her brother's death was an accident does not even begin to be the point. The point is that it was not unexpected. That is what was terrible then, what could not be made good, and that's what I felt I could see in Rolan Adams's father. The unquenchable anger of a man who has had his worst fear confirmed – that he lives in a place where he could not protect his child.

Before I leave, having Saturday-night reasons to be back in London, I say goodbye to Malik. And while his mates are all cooling out in the bar, Malik is alone in the main room, busy setting up a table on which to display campaign literature and organizing a fund-raising raffle. The campaign may be rolling now, but the man who's been pushing it is starting to look tired.

Weeks later yet, and starting to feel like too late, I'm watching 'Top of the Pops' in Alex's front room, waiting for Malik one more time. Michael Jackson is singing 'If you want to be my baby it don't matter if you're black or white'. His face is looking increasingly scary these days, luminous white and framed by hair that looks like it's made out of some fabric previously alien to this planet. But the kids are gathered round the TV and they're singing along, and here I am, surrounded by mixed-race children, in one of the few situations in which this thoroughly innocuous message song seems something like moving. And it strikes me that what Michael Jackson is engaged in is not really trying to be white but rather the more singular activity of trying to deracinate himself. Michael

Jackson's ambition is to be the authentic Brother From Another Planet – he does not want to join the white race, he wants to join the BambiLassiePeterPanStevenSpielberg race, and live happily ever after in neverneverDisneyAmerika.

I'm hoping to see Ronnie at last, the time before he ended up by blowing it out and anyway I'd come down with Malik's stomach bug, spent three days throwing up. But Malik's out on some kind of business, and so I'm back to cluttering up the living room. There's a ceaseless stream of people passing through. Among them this somewhat ferrety white guy with the inevitable badge of the true South Walian, the scrubby 'tache. He's called Darren. His wife is here too, tells us what she says she used to tell their little son, Tony, to explain his father's prolonged absence: 'Daddy's gone to work.' It turns out that's what all the mothers tell their kids when the men are inside. Alex knows what it's like, as do so many of the Butetown women, when the only real work open to their menfolk tends to be outside the law.

Darren's particular line, though, I discover after he's left, was heroin dealing. In fact, had I known, I could have had it from the, uh, horse's mouth, the ultimate refutation of the theory that there was something suspicious about the death of Martin Tucker, the sometime murder suspect. No way, says Malik, Darren dealt him the smack that killed him, it was just too pure, fact is Tucker wasn't the only one who turned blue that day, just the only one who didn't make it back.

After they've left I talk to Alex a little. Things are getting harder, she lost her temporary job at the bakery after missing a day while Gerry Conlon was down. Christmas is coming and the strains of trying to manage this campaign and run a family are starting to tell. There's no money, a huge phone bill, presents to buy and all the time the phone ringing with more requests for information, more journalists. All good news but not a living. Commitment is costing dear, not least because it has inhibited some of Malik's old-time money-making schemes.

By the time Malik finally returns from what seems to have

been some kind of wild-goose chase across Cardiff in search of the proverbial man about a dog, he's tired, and it's late, and trekking over to look for Ronnie is hardly on the agenda. Tomorrow though, he says, tomorrow we'll see Ronnie and tomorrow too we'll visit Dullah, they've brought him down to Cardiff Prison for Christmas.

It's around ten now so I call my friend Woody with whom I'm staying and arrange to meet him in the Packet at the bottom of Bute Street. The Packet is the least clannish of the Docks pubs, a big old boozer serving Brains beers, the fine local real ale disdained by most of the Docks boys in favour of strong lagers or shorts. But beer's popular enough in the Packet, it's mostly an old timers' place, recently done up with seafaring mementos and historical prints in an effort to catch the tourist trade, the Maritime Museum being just over the road. Tonight, though, there are no tourists to be seen, just a smattering of locals including a few of the White clan, this being one of their preferred watering holes.

Still, it's a quiet and comfortable place to sit and talk to Woody, who I've known since as far back as I can remember, growing up in the same village outside Cardiff. Woody bought a house in the Docks five years ago, amongst the first outsiders to do so. It made sense for him, he works on the edge of Butetown, making props for the Welsh National Opera, and his house has become a kind of way-station for impoverished operatic types.

Now he's doing his bit to try to combat the unchecked development proposed by the CBDC, which he sees as simply steamrolling over the needs of local people in the holy name of economic regeneration. Not that he's against regeneration, but he believes the community needs something more in the way of evidence that much of this so-called regeneration isn't just a piece of cynical property speculation. It's hard though, he says, to fight the development; people in the Docks seem possessed of a deep fatalism, a sense that there's nothing they can do. Their voices have never been listened to in the past so why bother complaining now?

The other day he's had a run-in on this subject with his neighbour Peggy Farrugia, sometime murder suspect and vociferous representative on behalf of 'the old Docks'. Woody had accused her of defeatism and she'd said nothing at first, then appeared at his door to harangue him – characteristic behaviour from a woman noted for keeping a shillelagh in the back of her brand new Golf car, which also features the entrancing bumper sticker: 'Insured by the Mafia – hit me and we hit you!'

Closing time and we head back to Woody's place on Windsor Esplanade, the very southern tip of the Docks. It's a two-hundred-yard walk made slightly longer because the road is being torn up and a new one laid, a feeder to the new link road that was once going to fly over this part of the Docks, but is now meant to tunnel under. Windsor Esplanade is a Victorian terrace looking out over the water. The sea captains used to live here, and turn-of-the-century photos show the houses with elegant balconies and horses and traps outside, men in top hats and elaborately dressed women. Now the balconies have gone, and the street has long been a slightly mouldering backwater. But there are signs of renewal: bohemians like Woody and his next-door neighbour may just be the inevitable harbingers of yuppification, but that remains to be seen. For the moment one can still hope that the presence of a little new blood raises the spirits of the street as a whole, without depriving it of its character, its relationship to the community.

In the morning, having spent the night swaddled in blankets against the sea wind, I look out over the mud flats to the Bristol Channel ahead of me; and away from me, to my right across the dull water of the bay, I can see the beginnings of Penarth, the Edwardian resort just along the coast beyond the south-western tip of the bay. The view as it is now can look anything from bleak to beautiful, depending on the weather and the mood of the beholder, but it always looks like the end of something – a seafaring era perhaps. It has that kind of abandoned beauty that has lately been somewhat over-represented in photo spreads in Sunday magazines and such places.

And I reckon that this is the first stage of an invidious double whammy. First, the sites of working-class history are speedily to be reduced to aesthetically forlorn imagery. Second, when such imagery inevitably falls out of fashion, this will be allowed to imply that what it represented – working-class history – is also unfashionable, does not need to be remembered.

Being dangled before us now, in place of history, is the prospect of a conventional pleasantness: a marina, a reclaimed park, a nice new Barratt-type estate or two. Gone will be the opportunity to indulge in nostalgic tristesse, and gone too will be a whole spectrum of protected marine birdlife. But maybe there will be prosperity, a new town by the sea, and maybe that will be better. Maybe.

A van arrives in front of the terrace. The back of the van opens up and reveals it to be a fruit and veg store on wheels. A cheery Len Fairclough/Pete Beale-type market trader leaps into action and the street acquires a certain amount of animation. It's something I remember from growing up in the country – men coming round in vans to sell food to people who didn't then have the transport to get them to the Sainsbury's superstores, which didn't exist then anyway. I doubt that there'll be much of a place for such activity in the new-look bay either, but what the hell – progress!

Late breakfast at Babs's Bistro. Read the paper and chomp through sausage, bacon, egg, beans, fried slice and black pudding, bread and butter on the side, plus a cup of tea, all for £1.85, and, refreshed to the point of imminent heart seizure, I head over to Malik's.

Alex and Malik are in the kitchen looking exhausted, but there's good news. 'Panorama' have called up this morning: they're definitely going to make a programme on the case, and they'll have people coming down next week. Malik is pleased but preoccupied; he's still looking for someone, him and Lloyd are going up to Ely. A guy comes round, says where were you last night, you never called; I was sleeping by the phone, man, you never called. The conversation moves upstairs, then Malik comes back down. He's got business to attend to, but suggests that I go to the prison with Alex and Stephanie, Rashid's missus.

So I wait with Alex, watching daytime TV until Stephanie, a sharp light-skinned woman, shows up and we catch a cab to the prison. The cab's late so by the time we get there the waiting room is full, full of young women and children with the occasional old couple and a few stray brothers. It's like Monday-morning dole office, not enough chairs, air of insti-tutionalized neglect, No Smoking signs barely visible through the fug, and so on. But the clientele are notably better dressed. The women tend to look like they're about to go clubbing, disconcertingly made-up in the winter daylight, hair elabor-ately teased, and most likely permed and dyed blonde; or, the upcoming look for villains' girlfriends, sleekly bobbed and glossily hennaed. It's less depressing than a dole office – I have the sense that most people here live lives in which jail is no more than a fact of life, in which Daddy going to work is no great surprise; so the talk is lively, centring round clubbing uptown. Sharp girls with babies come up to Stephanie and talk about last weekend's rave, and eventually it's our turn to go through the security door into the visiting hall.

The hall is a big room full of desks, prisoners on one side of the desk, visitors on the other, but they can hug and hold hands and buy cups of tea and sweets and cans of Coke. And there's Yusef, heavy-set and throwing his arms around Alex and Stephanie. Me he regards with fairly amiable suspicion as soon as he hears I'm a journalist, but he shakes my hand anyway before getting down to a serious family row on the subject of what his dealings should be with his ex, Jackie. Stephanie and Alex are telling him not to see her, that he can't trust her, that if she sees him she is capable of, for instance, telling the police that he confessed to her, so he's safer not seeing her. What about my kids? he says. We'll bring them, not her. OK, he agrees.

I just have time to tell him a little about what I'm doing and he tells me that he has been writing the history of his growing up in Butetown. We agree to talk more next time and it's back to family business till we leave. While we're there, though, the friendliness of the screws is striking. Yusef confirms this, says they know about the case, know something's not right. And certainly that's the impression I get: they're not treating him like a man who has butchered an innocent woman. Within the prison system, it seems, people generally know the score; prisoners and screws alike know who has been fitted up, who's a villain and who's a psycho, who's a nonce and who shouldn't be in there at all. It's just out here that justice is blind. Perhaps juries made up of prisoners and prison officers would be likelier to get things right.

From the jail I walk the back way to Butetown with Alex and Stephanie, cross the footbridge over the railway line, along the industrial waste of Tyndall Street. As we walk they're talking about the shit that's going to come down when Rashid is let out of jail for the weekend soon, the scores that'll be settled. It's another world they're in, foreign enough that there's no need for another language to guard against my hearing. I simply don't know what's going on.

Nor do I know what's going on when we get back to the house. Lloyd is slumped in a chair in front of the snooker, hat pulled down over his eyes. Malik looks more drained than ever, and is talking into the phone. Now the two of them have to go over to Splott. Ely was no good but they've got another lead in whatever chase they're on. They are going to find the guy's mother's place. But they'll run me down to the station on the way.

In the car there's the feeling that some shit really is coming down: Rashid coming out, the Abdullahi family in full feud, Dullah talking about a hunger strike, and Christmas coming down like a bastard. And still they're carrying this thing on with no money. They've got 'Panorama' coming down and that is pure good news. They have magicked this campaign into being but they are tired now and it is becoming clear how much may rest on this programme: if the rest of Cardiff/Wales/ Britain says that native sons Tony and Dullah could have done this thing, then that will be that. This community – or the people at its hustling heart – has given its not-lightly-given backing to this, and if it fails then I feel that the Bay Development will roll over the community.

But if they succeed, if the city/country says that the police, the judge, the jury were wrong, then just maybe the self-belief can be found to restore the real spirit of the bay, not let it be replaced by Theme Park Tiger Bay. That's what I think as I get on the train back to London, leaving Malik and Lloyd to their wanderings.

Nine o'clock in the evening, three days after Christmas, on the first day of the sales, I'm sat at the bar of the Custom House, wishing I was back home watching festive reruns of 'Only Fools and Horses'.

Not that it's not festive in here, mind, the place has only just finished singing along to 'The Power of Love', and no doubt someone will be putting 'I'm Too Sexy' on the jukebox one more time before too long. And it doesn't look like most of the women in here are likely to be working much tonight. Certainly the group sitting behind me next to the door to the toilets are too pissed for anything except more drinking. There are a couple of younger women, though, sitting to my left over by the pool table who look ready for action, in fact one of them's just now passing her drink to a pool player, asking them to hold it till she returns and heading out into the night, in search of business. She's perhaps surprisingly attractive, a dark, long-haired girl with fine bones, but her eyes and the set of her mouth have a hardness, an impenetrable cynicism unlike anything essayed on celluloid by Julia Roberts.

But, Jesus, is it depressing in here, there are some falling-down drunks by the door, the inevitable parade of taxi drivers asking for people too drunk to remember they ordered a cab, elderly boys from the Valleys trying to prevent their mate from starting a fight or throwing up over anyone – the place is full of folks who never intend to finish drinking up, because they don't have any homes they'd ever want to go to. The jukebox is playing, of all things, Salt'n'Pepa's 'Let's Talk about Sex'. Which is bizarre: you might have thought that songs about work would be less than welcome, but no, it's going down a treat. A mass singalong suggests some kind of subversion of the song, but I'm at a loss to know what sort of subversion.

Or maybe I do know, maybe it's that the atmosphere in this place, while overwhelmingly depressing and defeated, is subversive in its flagrant disregard for any of the polite conventions of modern life. The Custom House, seen from that perspective, is a shrunken freeport, a wide-open saloon gone terminally to seed, a place where raddled lesbians and black macho dealer/pimps are united in their failure and their bravado.

And I don't want to be here tonight. I've spent the day getting nowhere. Malik and Lloyd are running round town with 'Panorama', plus another documentary crew, this time from 'Wales This Week'. They've got no time. Alex sounds like a ghost as she tells me this, trying to make herself heard above the noise of the Nintendo games console that she and Malik have somehow managed to get the kids for Christmas. Everyone else I try to contact is out of the office until the New Year and so here I am in one place where the denizens are people for whom cold turkey is not something to pop in a sandwich on Boxing Day.

Just as I'm screwing up enough foolhardiness to try and interview the collection of pissed-up superannuated hookers behind me, there's the arrival of the hardman posse, another of the unmistakable shaven-headed Actie clan amidst them. The pub quiets down perceptibly as they enter, look around and walk to the bar to order bottles of Pils. They stand around in the middle of the pub for a while, owning the space, conversing a little. While they're there I start to make a move to the table behind me but the barmaid calls me back with an urgent hiss. I've already told her that I'm a journalist and discovered that she's new here herself. I'd wait till those boys have gone, she says, so I order another can of Breaker, and watch the guys drink up their Pils and leave, giving me the strong sense that there was some purpose to their visit – collecting money maybe – but whatever it was I'd missed it.

This turns out to be about par for the course this night. When I finally make it over to the old tart table and explain what I'm doing I'm rewarded first with a 'Sorry, love, I'm too pissed to talk' from a middle-aged black woman and then with a stream of abuse from her more voluble tablemates.

'Show us your press card,' says Georgette, the black lesbian with the locks and the leonine countenance.

'He doesn't have a card. He just wants to take photos, the pervert,' says a Scots woman with the blonde mane and the slabs of make-up battling with the effects of a too hard life.

'Fuck off, fuck off, fuck off,' say several people at once.

So I do my best. I explain that I'm writing a book on the Lynette White case, that I'm not a hard news journalist, that I don't carry a card. This doesn't help much, but I battle on and mention Lloyd and Malik and that gives me a little pause in the otherwise continuous barrage of abuse, in which to try and explain what I'm doing and offer them a say.

There's just a hint that this might be getting somewhere when all of a sudden there's a hand on my shoulder. It's the landlord and he is not pleased. 'I want a word with you,' he says. 'In private.' He assists me through the door into the passage to the toilets and lounge bar (defunct). 'What the fuck do you think you're doing,' he says, 'coming in here and mentioning that name? You could get yourself killed.' He says this in tones that suggest that that would be a bad thing only inasmuch as it would involve him in considerable hassle with the police. 'If one of those boys who were in just now had heard you, you'd be in trouble. So finish your drink and get out. I don't want to see your face in here again, ever.'

I return to my drink and the women chime up. What makes you so sure they didn't do it then? And the landlord decides to modify his strictures. Forget the finishing the drink part.

Out. Now. The women watch me go with the kind of regret lions show when deprived of Christians.

And I'm out of there. It takes a moment for me to realize the enormity of this: I've been thrown out of the Custom House. I've actually been expelled from a place in which there is virtually no level of violence, drunkenness or lewdness that would not be tolerated, a pub in which, and just for instance, I have seen a man bodily thrown through a window by his mates, without anyone being more formally ejected. It's extraordinary and it begs the question: why does everyone in the Custom House evince such hysteria at the name of Lynette White? Why should it be dangerous to ask questions about her? Who do they think cares? Why should the Actie clan be bothered if their boys have already been acquitted? What do the hustlers think is going on?

Or is the fear displaced? The death of Lynette White surely has a touch of 'there but for the grace of God go I' to it and to fix her death on to the local badmen at least prevents it from being the work of an unknown maniac who is still at large. So maybe that's it – better blame it on the devil you know, too frightening to contemplate the devil you don't – if you're going to stand out there in the cold for another night, get in any car with any man, then drive to an empty place and turn your back to them in the front seat.

Me, I'm sitting in the front seat and heading out of town to my parents' house: cold ham and turkey, another box of chocolates, why not? Another world.

NINE

The Appeal and After

We're into the New Year of 1992, with the appeal date still to be fixed, and the stress has told. I'm playing pool with Malik in the skittles room of the Wyndham and we're waiting for a friend of his to get ready to talk to me about her sometime friend Lynette White. Before we came in here we went round to Angela Psaila's flat. I pressed the intercom, asked if she wanted to talk and she told me to fuck off. I suggested she might like to put her side of the case and she told me she'd had enough of people like me coming round and harassing her, so would I just bog off.

While this altercation was going on, a young black guy came out of the block of flats, listened to me arguing and offered the open door to me so I could go up and see this person who clearly didn't want to see me. I couldn't see much mileage in that so I rejoined Malik in the car and adjourned to the pub for a couple of games of pool.

Last night Malik was telling me about 'Panorama', who've now been down for a month, expense accounts blazing, Tom Mangold in command, a couple of BBC smoothies riding shotgun. They've been running round town talking to everyone. Psaila has given them no joy but they've been flirting with Leanne Vilday. She's been accepting twenty pounds an hour to sit in pubs and Chinese restaurants with them, teetering, on the edge of coming clean. Malik and Lloyd have been riding the gravy terrain for all they're worth: stick next to the man from the BBC if you fancy a drink or a bite to eat. They've been having a good time too, stories abound about taking the Panorama team out raving and the apparatchiks letting their hair down.

But this lunchtime Malik's down. He's under all manner of domestic pressure. He's talking about splitting up with Alex. The latest domestic development involves the mother of his other child, who's taken to parading the infant down by the school playground, in front of Malik's and Alex's daughters, saying look, here's your sister. The girls are upset and Malik for once doesn't know what to do. Meanwhile he's got problems with his flat and now there's a rift opening up with John Actie, who has started up his own freelance campaign, organizing raves as benefits for himself alone. The fragility of the defence coalition is starting to become uncomfortably apparent.

By six o'clock I've exchanged the unvarnished, rougher-than-ready surrounds of the Wyndham for the faux 'Cheers' charm of Henry's Bar in Park Place, just off the main pedestrianized shopping drag of Queen Street and opposite the former site of the Park Hall Cinema which used to have the biggest screen in Cardiff and where I was as a child comprehensively terrified by the Cinemascope tidal wave that opened a film called *Krakatoa East of Java*. Henry's is the kind of somewhat schizophrenic place that seems to be sprouting all over Britain. It has pretensions to being a cocktail-bar-cum-eatery with full table service, but its clientele think it's a pub and accordingly order their drinks at the bar, which means the place has slightly crotchety waiting staff standing round in the vain hope that someone will order their drinks from them.

I'm talking to Leila Attfield, waiting for Stuart Hutton to arrive. The two of them work for Huttons, John Actie's solicitors throughout the trial, and Ronnie Actie's too for a while. Leila seems to be Huttons' Butetown specialist. She's from the Docks herself, and tells me that this case took over her life, will still not leave her alone. In particular she's still hurt by the behaviour of Ronnie who ditched Huttons in between the two trials, in a welter of paranoid accusations.

Then Stuart arrives. He's the boss and, like Leila, he's a stocky, determined-looking individual as well as another whom this case just won't let alone. When we finish our interview we spend a while speculating as to what the hell did happen in that room. Hutton hypothesizes some kind of murderous gay and lesbian alliance. Leila propounds the notion that the murder may have been committed elsewhere, that there was not enough blood in the murder room. Or maybe there's a link to the killing of Geraldine Polk . . .

And so it goes on. I'm left with a sense that this case has scarred the lives, wounded the charms of everyone associated with it and that the people involved want the murder to have something extraordinary about it, need it to be the product of a conspiracy or whatever – it has simply taken too much out of too many people's lives for them to accept it as just another, too common, aberrance. And all of us know it's not over yet.

Six months later, a week or so after the announcement of the appeal date I'm sitting with Malik and Lloyd in the Packet. They're both on edge, restless with anticipation and needing something to do. The campaign has done its work now. The job's in the hands of the lawyers. There's this sense that frantic activity is going on on the legal front – the police have finally granted access to a whole mass of paperwork relating to the case, Jackie Harris has apparently made a statement recanting her original evidence, things are on the move . . .

And yet here are Lloyd and Malik, prime movers in this whole business, without whom there would more than likely not be an appeal, and they're feeling like spare parts. So we're in the pub in the late afternoon wondering what might go wrong. Everyone's saying that it's going to be a formality next week. *The Voice* has even printed a front-page story saying 'Cardiff Three Home for Christmas'. And that all feels like bad juju, tempting fate and so forth.

So rather than talk about that we're having an argument about racism. Lloyd is saying that this whole case is just another example of the racist British system in action, while Malik leans more to the view that it's not so much a black thing as a Butetown thing. We move on, talking about how they first became aware of British racism. They're both in agreement that, as long as they were in Butetown, there was no problem, but when they went out into the wider world there sure as hell was a problem. The funny thing is that back then it was Malik who was the militant. He remembers when he went to secondary school out of Butetown, at Fitzalan, he felt constantly under attack and so distinctly hostile towards white folks. Lloyd was plucked out of the community to attend the semi-private Bishop of Llandaff's school and says he never had a problem, was even able to joke about the race business.

Now their experience has bent them out of shape in different ways. Lloyd simply sees the sheer bloody injustice of what has been done to his brother and the fact that this injustice has happened in a country where black people are given an over-whelmingly worse deal than whites by the legal system, and he sees this so clearly that he has reached the point at which, rhetorically at least, he'd just like to leave this Babylonian shithole behind. Yet Malik has accepted that only in inte-gration and combined action lie the possibility of changing things. He hopes.

And, hopes in hand, it's time to go. Malik and Lloyd head off in the interminable and mysterious pursuit of 'business' and I stop to make a phone call. As I finish the call and head out of the pub my arm is caught by a woman who's been standing at the bar. She's red-faced with anger and afternoon drinking and she wants to know who I am. Am I a reporter? Why was I drinking with Lloyd and Malik?

Well, yes, I say. I'm writing about the case, you know. Yes, she says, she does know. She's Aileen, Lynette's auntie. And how do I know those boys didn't do it, eh? How did I know and what do Lloydie and Malik think they're doing anyway drinking in this pub when they know her family drinks here? And don't they know what it's done to us? Don't they know? And you reporters, all you say is prostitute prostitute prosti-tute. She was a lovely girl, what she did was her own business. Why doesn't anyone ask us what we think? Why are you always talking to them?

Reeling slightly I say, well, surely I would like to hear your side of the story. But this only serves to further upset Aileen. No, she says, she's too frightened and no way could they trust any of us bastard journalists. They helped one once and he just told a lot of lies. He didn't know. I knew her, she was a beautiful little girl. Not like that stupid photo they always put in the papers. Not like that. And then she fumbles in her handbag, pulls out her purse and extracts a photo.

The picture is of a little blonde girl, about eleven years of age. And Aileen's right, Lynette doesn't look like the picture that's always in the papers. She looks happy.

As I leave, Aileen's crying into her drink and I'm backing off, saying sorry, sorry for what I'm not quite sure. For intruding into private pain partly, for taking that little blonde girl's life and exposing it to the acid glare of publicity. All that and more.

Monday morning, nine thirty a.m., I'm sitting on a bench in the Appeal Courts with a cup of coffee and a tuna sandwich. Outside the building there are various Trot hawkers attempting to catch a ride on the Cardiff Three bandwagon. Inside not much is happening.

The notice board says the case is going to be heard in Court 4, the Lord Chief Justice of England's Court, so clearly someone somewhere is taking this business seriously. Lined up with Lord Justice Taylor will be Lords Popplewell and Laws – a name so appropriate as to defy wordplay. But when I make my way upstairs there seems to be another case entirely going on. No one I recognize is in either the dock or the public seats so I go back into the corridor and wait for something to happen.

First, the press arrives. Heading the charge are the two daily newspaperpersons who've done most to promote the campaign, the *Independent*'s Rachel Borrill and the *Guardian*'s Duncan Campbell. Next up a woman from the *Socialist Worker* and a man from the *Western Mail*. More cups of coffee, standing around and small talk follow. The court empties out and new teams of legal types gather. Suddenly the solemnity is

punctured by a crew of newcomers swarming down the corridor towards us. Track-suited, dreadlocked, pony-tailed or
permed, bad boys, soul girls and roots radicals, the Cardiff
posse has arrived.

They're in buoyant mood for the most part – the exceptions,
though, are the principal players; Lloyd, Malik and Alex are
all wearing suits and looking anxious. Pauline Abdullahi is
here too and the tension is getting to her. Still, greetings are
exchanged and then the ushers open the door to the public.
Family first, they say, and thirty or so of the Cardiff contingent
press towards the door. That's the public seating full and for
a moment things threaten to turn ugly as there are still forty
of us left outside. But the ushers announce that there's seating
in the gallery and off we're led, filing up a perilously dark and
narrow spiral stairway.

Peering down from the front row centre of the gallery, the
judges are dead ahead of me overlooking the court. Immediately in front of them is the clerk, to the clerk's left are the
press benches. Facing this lot, and more or less underneath
the gallery, are several long rows of benches. The front three
benches are packed with legal types, the last two full of family.
And stuck over on the far right corner, there's the dock.

But Stephen, Tony and Yusef aren't there. Instead there's
a pallid white man with glasses and a suit. Turns out that
there's another case to be heard first. It doesn't take long. The
pallid white guy turns out to be an eighties whizz kid who
founded a Yorkshire investment empire on the ever-popular
bedrock of misappropriated pension funds. The empire went
belly-up with around £4 million in debts and the subsequent
investigation succeeded in nailing three or four of the princi-
pals for fraud. Our man was evidently the prime mover and
had received five years for his pains. He was here though to
appeal against the severity of this sentence. His counsel
pointed out that our man had pleaded guilty (albeit only
minutes before his trial was due to begin), had not done it for
personal gain (though he had accepted a modest salary of
£75,000 a year), and had been abandoned by his wife and

children (she had returned to her native South Africa). This last piece of information loses any residual sympathy up here in the gallery, not that there was too much in the first place, most of whom figuring that, if they were involved in any criminal activity to the tune of four million quid, they would more than likely be looking at a lot more than five years in an open prison.

Still Justice Taylor, while not looking overly impressed, agrees that, given a likely maximum of a six-year sentence for this offence if the case had gone to trial and produced a guilty verdict, the discount for pleading guilty was indeed insufficient and reduces the sentence to four years.

Another few minutes, a further shuffling of legal types, and it's show time. Tony and Yusef are led into the dock (without Miller at this stage as his appeal is technically separate). No sooner have they identified themselves than David Elfer QC, returning to the fray for the prosecution, is up on his feet.

And he wants to put things off. Mr Abdullahi's counsel has supplied him with a whole bunch of new affidavits just ten minutes ago, he complains. Among them is one from Jackie Harris apparently retracting her original evidence. How can he possibly be expected to deal with such evidence so speedily? Just to obtain a transcript of the original trial for comparison purposes will take at least a fortnight. Oh no, there's no way he can be expected to go ahead now.

This seems pretty remarkable to me. One might have thought that a transcript of the original trial would have been obtained automatically for the appeal but apparently not. And clearly the age of the fax machine has not had too profound an impact on the Crown Prosecution Service, if it takes them a fortnight to produce a document. Justice Taylor doesn't seem too impressed by this either, but neither is he very pleased with the defence for leaving it to the last moment. So he calls time out for the lawyers to try to thrash something out. It's twelve o'clock now, we'll adjourn till two.

Back outside and everyone's spirits are dampened. Malik is sitting with his mother in an alcove, Lloyd is looking ready to punch a hole in the venerable walls. Both of them are wound up beyond belief and the prospect of a delay of God knows how many more months is just unbearable. Over the road in the pub it's not much better. Knots of supporters stand around marvelling at the pricing policies of London pubs, and everyone's wondering if today's just going to be a painful anticlimax. I'm sitting watching Lloyd and Sharon work their way through a plate of fish and chips, when Malik appears, says he's heard that the lawyers have agreed on a restart on Friday. Now they're going to see whether Taylor will go for it. Friday. Could be worse.

Back in court Elfer stands up and says that just maybe, with luck, perhaps something might be managed by Friday. A transcript had, after all, already been ordered and should be here soon, but no guarantees . . . Taylor is singularly unimpressed by this. Well, he points out, if we start with Miller's evidence we're unlikely to be ready for Abdullahi's case much before Friday, are we? So, he says, in a tone that brooks no further argument, let's get on with it.

The appeal's under way. Stephen Miller is brought out into the dock, looking natty in a green wool blazer and dark shirt, in mild contrast to Yusef's and Tony's sober suits. And Michael Mansfield, stellar defence QC, is out of the starting blocks.

He begins with an outline of what he's going to do. He recaps the case, casually dropping a small bombshell in the process, before announcing that he intends to start by demonstrating that Miller's confession was obtained by unfair and oppressive questioning by the police. This, he warns us, will be a fairly lengthy process as there were thirteen hours of taped interviews and we will need to hear quite a lot of those interviews in order to understand just how oppressive and insidious the police questioning was. So time to settle back on the benches, folks.

The bombshell Mansfield dropped in passing was the revelation that the police had had a suspect whose blood type matched the bloodstains found on Lynette's jeans – a man Mansfield referred to only as Mr X, before promising that we would hear more of him. This information gives us something to ponder on as the day drifts to an end with Mansfield, Elfer and Taylor debating as to which tapes the defence wanted to focus on and which the prosecution, which tapes should be listened to in full in court, which ones should be listened to by the judges out of court, and which should simply be summarized.

And that's it for day one. Words of encouragement are shouted at the men in the dock as they are led away, and then it's back on the coach for the support crew, tired but thankful that things are at last under way.

Next morning it's a smaller crowd that's arrived by minibus. Malik and Alex have stayed at home, exhausted, but Lloyd is here, and Rosie and Wayne, and Des, Steve, Kermit . . . And Miller's family are here again, a matriarchal clan: mother, sister, grandmother, aunt. Their demeanour contrasts somewhat with the Butetown crowd: they seem altogether more fatalistic, more resigned to the injustice of life.

But things are looking up for their boy this morning. Mansfield digresses from the interview tapes to tell us more about Mr X. Not only did this gent provide a matching blood sample, but he was a client of Lynette's, had a conviction for rape, was described as a psychopath by his doctor and, eerily, had been attacked himself by a prostitute armed with a machete, who inflicted cuts on his throat and wrists – where Lynette had received the most brutal cuts.

Mr Elfer for the prosecution then explained that Mr X had been eliminated because his blood did not provide an exactly perfect match for the stain on the sock, and his DNA profile was different to that lifted from the stain on the wall. Which would have seemed a more satisfactory explanation if the police had not then gone on to prosecute five men who matched none of the bloodstains . . .

This was the good bit, the rest of the day dragged on interminably as Mansfield painstakingly advanced his thesis that the police had used good cop/bad cop routines to wear down Miller's resistance and persuade him that he had no option but to go along with them in constructing a kind of partial confession, in which he would admit to witnessing, but not being involved in, some part of the killing. The key breakthrough, so Mansfield maintained, was achieved by driving a wedge into Miller's consistent denials.

This wedge was the 'blocked up' hypothesis. The police hammered away at the idea that Miller might have been too out of it on drink and drugs to remember what happened. This too he denied repeatedly, but eventually he agreed that it was at least possible in the abstract to be too blocked up to know what you are doing. This was the first crack in his armour and the police knew it and they drove a coach and horses through it. 'One could be that out of it' became 'you were that out of it'. And then another step, 'you could not remember who you met' became 'you met these four or five or six people'. And finally, 'You were so blocked up that you remember nothing' became 'you saw your girlfriend getting hacked to pieces'.

This is a solid and convincing thesis but hearing it one more time and at such length means that the coffee bar gets a fair amount of repeat business from onlookers trying to keep awake. And here the talk is mostly about Mr X – who is he and why isn't he in jail? The first question is answered easily enough; a journalist puts a name to the sobriquet and says he was one of the semi-vagrants who were living in the porta-kabins round the corner from the Custom House. As for why he wasn't locked up, God and/or ex-CID Chief John Williams would be the best bet for an answer. And neither of them was prepared to risk imbibing the industrial fluid emitted by the Appeal Court café's automatic drinks dispenser.

After Tuesday's attritional tedium, expectations were lowered a little for Wednesday. Arriving slightly late, I bump into Malik outside the courtroom. It's his turn today, Lloyd's just too wound up to come. Malik's just been talking to his brother's solicitor, Bernard De Maid, and Yusef can have a visit at lunchtime. Be downstairs at one if I want to come too.

Inside, the courtroom is packed ready to listen to Tape 7, the one the defence are rumoured to be banking on to get Miller out of jail. I squeeze on to the end of a bench next to Wayne and Rosie and listen.

What Tape 7 consists of mostly is two coppers shouting at Stephen Miller, pounding him with accusations of involvement while his voice, high-pitched with fear, repeats 'I wasn't there, I wasn't there'.

The court is silent, straining to make sense of the swirl of noise. Miller, sitting in the dock, is visibly upset, crying at first, then sitting with his head bowed as he relives the deliberate humiliation wreaked on him by two men he was powerless to stop.

At the end of it Lord Justice Taylor is clearly struck by what he's heard. First he says that this has proved 'just how important it is to hear the tape. One could read the transcript without getting any flavour at all'. Then he inquires as to what Miller's solicitor was doing during this interrogation. Mansfield tells us that the solicitor, while accepting the police tactics at the time, admitted, on hearing the tape again before the original trial, that he should have stepped in.

It's a tape that has since been characterized as horrifying. In truth, for anyone used to watching endless cop movies it's pretty tame stuff. There's no physical violence, little swearing even, just two officers working up a head of furious steam as they browbeat an exhausted suspect with continual accusations of involvement in a particularly brutal murder. But then that's one of fiction's falsehoods. No one needs beatings and electrodes and truth drugs to elicit a confession. Leave anyone alone for long enough in a darkened room and they'll confess to whatever you like. Put a suggestible young man in a police station for hours and hours on end, with teams of policemen taking turns to yell accusations at him and he – and more than likely me or you – will soon start trying to cooperate.

This is of course the point that Mr Mansfield is making. Tape 7, he says, is where the police broke Stephen Miller's will, where they scared him – by making him believe that this would go on and on and on – to the point at which he stopped believing that just being innocent would be enough to save him.

The proof of the pudding came in Tape 8. Ostensibly Tape 8 is the reverse of Tape 7. The two bullying officers are replaced by two pleasant chaps who just want Stephen to help them out with a couple of things. In fact they're positively concerned about him, worried that he might be drinking too much, or taking too many drugs, might not remember what he'd been doing sometimes. And there it is, the opening for a confession that wouldn't really be a confession. If Stephen Miller could just agree that he might possibly sometimes get so out of it that he would not be able to remember what he'd done the night before, then surely 13 February 1988 might have been one of those days and thus, if the police were to make a few suggestions as to what might have happened that night, then he, at least, would be unable to contradict them.

For a while Miller resisted. Yes, he drank. Yes, he took drugs, smoked hash, black, cocaine. But, no, he didn't get too out of it to remember what he was doing. (This is an account that his friends don't doubt. After all, it is only really alcohol – and maybe acid or heroin – that promotes that kind of memory loss, not really ganja, certainly not cocaine. Furthermore, drink was the least of Miller's vices: he's a two or three brandies man, not a sixteen bottles of Pils headcase.) But in their own way the relief team, the nice cops, are just as insistent as the bad cops, who are anyway held up as a threat any time Miller tries to clam up. This works well enough and each time it's tried Miller pleads with the nice guys to continue.

And soon enough he realizes that the price for being left alone with the nice guys is his continued cooperation. Give them just a little something to keep them happy. At the end of Tape 8 he sticks a toe in the water a little further, realizing that once he'd started there's no going back. Yes, he said, maybe he did get so out of it that he couldn't remember what happened. 'That's right. Most probably,' he agreed, as he would so many times over the succeeding hours of questioning interview.

That's all for the morning. It's an early and long lunch today. Also Lord Justice Taylor announces that he has an engagement on Friday and would like to take that day off if possible. Elfer and Mansfield um and ah a bit, and off we go to lunch, figuring that a second week looks inevitable with only this afternoon and tomorrow left and Mansfield only on Tape 8. Over in the pub though, the *Independent*'s Rachel Borrill reckons we've had the breakthrough, that Taylor's reaction to Tape 7 means that the Cardiff Three are home free. Some people agree. Some people cross their fingers, mindful of the fact that that's what most insiders thought at the original trial.

Meanwhile there's dissension in the ranks of the Cardiff crew. Malik has gone to see Yusef and his absence provokes a flurry of complaint, mostly from Kermit who drove the minibus all the way up and was looking forward to parking it on a meter around the corner from the Law Courts, but was instructed by Malik that there was no money available for such a purpose and would he mind driving on to Hackney, parking the van outside the restricted zone and getting a bus back to the Strand. Kermit therefore is feeling a little undervalued and threatening to withdraw his services tomorrow. A pint of lager calms him down though and soon enough he, Pepsi and Paulie Paris are engaged in an edifying debate as to how best to take maximum advantage of the satellite television services for the minimum amount of money.

Back in the courtroom café there's more grumbling. It's an odd, strained time, things are looking up, people are whispering that it might finish today, but no one's sure.

In the afternoon Mansfield develops his theme. The police good cop/bad cop tactics paid off in Tapes 7 and 8. They made the crucial breakthrough in Tape 8 and they stuck with the good cops who steadily widened the breach in Miller's defence. Soon it was taken as read that Miller had been totally out of it on the night of the murder and Leanne Vilday's statements were being read out to jog his memory. A pattern soon developed whereby the police would outline a Vilday scenario and then ask Miller if that could have been the way it was. Miller would start out by denying it and then – if necessary after a little reminder that there were a couple of bad cops just straining at the leash to get at him – agree that 'Yeah, it could have happened. Most probably'.

First he agreed to seeing a group of men outside the flats. Then inside the flat. Then in the room with Lynette. Then, crucially, in the room with him and Lynette, and doing violence to Lynette. Then, at last, in the room and murdering Lynette.

Still, there were problems though. Giving identity to this group of men was a problem. Miller was clearly reluctant to name names. But here too the cops wore him down. Persuasively they pointed out that he was a London boy and they were Docks boys and he was never going to be one of them. Be a bright boy, they implied, shop them before they shop you. And after a while, sure enough, he remembered that he most probably did know the guys who were there – the murderer, Tony Paris, and his cohorts: Dullah, John and Ronnie Actie and a couple of white guys standing on the stairs (one of the many deeply peculiar features of the initial prosecution was the complete unconcern shown at the fact that the main witness referred throughout to these two white guys who were never identified or explained away).

More troublesome still was getting any circumstantial detail into Miller's confession. Mansfield neatly demonstrated the way in which the police – faced with a man ready to make a partial confession but pitifully ignorant of the events he was about to confess to – managed to feed titbits to Miller for him to repeat back to them. And when the going really got rough they resorted to getting out the map.

The map was a plan of 7 James Street. Its ostensible purpose was to refresh Stephen Miller's stoned memory. Its practical purpose to make sure his story at least approximated to the known facts – whereabouts in which room Lynette's body had been found, and so on.

So the afternoon was mostly spent listening to Mansfield develop this argument, showing the way in which, in the course of Tapes 9 to 13, the police officers gradually shepherded Miller into providing a roughly coherent account of the killing of Lynette White.

Then it was Elfer's turn. He suggested that the judge should listen to Tapes 14 and 15, in which, he would argue, Stephen Miller confessed, clearly and without undue pressure, to the murder of his then girlfriend, Lynette White. This had to be Elfer's best chance. It was Tape 14 that had been crucial in the first trial. The jury had asked the judge to allow them to listen to a section of the tape immediately before they returned the guilty verdict against Abdullahi, Paris and Miller (presumably in defiance of the rule that a confession should not be taken as evidence against anyone except the confessor). The key section is a passage in which a barely coherent Miller is babbling something about Tony Paris stabbing and stabbing.

Listening to it now in court, it is clear how well Mansfield has laid his groundwork. For what must have seemed to the jury to be the raving of a guilty man haunted by his sins, now seems clearly the distressed mumbling of a man desperately trying to concoct a story vivid enough for the police to accept and let him out of this awful jail cell, the way they said they would if he could just help them enough.

Not a confession then but the sound of a frightened child trying to remember the lines of a playscript he's never learned. The jury's misreading of what they heard must surely be the product of a society unable or unwilling to see a black man as frightened rather than frightening.

Still, at the end of Tape 14 the mood in the public gallery was anxious – the tape had done the damage once, might it not do the same again? Further confusion was spread by the last exchange of the day. Taylor once again raised the matter of whether they would need the Friday and asked Mansfield how long he expected to take to present the remainder of his case. Mansfield then asked for permission to call two expert witnesses to provide further testimony in connection with Miller's statements – to discuss the language used (whether it resembled Miller's normal speech or words put into his mouth) and the psychological impact of such questioning upon such a personality.

Lord Justice Taylor replied with words to the effect that if Mr Mansfield really felt that necessary then he could go ahead, but personally he felt that the tapes were more or less self-explanatory and expert glosses not really necessary. So it looked like Taylor had made his mind up. But which way?

Outside, some welcome distraction is provided by the news that Charles and Di are to separate. It's the curse of the Cardiff Three: the day they were convicted they were shovelled off the front page by the news of Margaret Thatcher's resignation. Now media coverage of the appeal looks set to be lost in a welter of variously uninformed royal speculation.

Next morning, Thursday, things seem to have slowed down again. Tapes 16 and 17 are summarized, then Tape 18 is listened to in full, so we can all bear witness to the unedifying sound of two police officers persuading Miller to go through a couple more cartwheels and change his story to encompass the latest seismic shift in the testimony of Vilday and Psaila which has them both in the room being forced to cut the body. Miller has never mentioned these two before but now all of a sudden he has to remember that he assisted in the forcing at knife point of these two girls to cut the dying body of their friend. And after a while, and a few judicious threats, he does indeed so remember. 'Most probably.'

Midway through the tape I slip out for a cup of coffee and run into David Webster, Tony's solicitor. He's pleased with the way things are going, though cautious as ever, and already starting to worry about what will happen to the Three if they get out. He's got the highest hopes for Tony his client, who, he believes, has grown up as a person while in prison. But faced with a niggardly compensation scheme, that can render its recipient ineligible for any state benefit for years, he worries.

Back to the court room, Tape 18 finishes and Tape 19 is summarized. That's the end of the tapes. Now Mansfield asks if he can call at least one expert witness, the psychologist. Taylor looks at his fellow judges, they talk amongst themselves for a moment, then Taylor says they need a moment to discuss something. They absent themselves and I sit back and look around the court, realizing all of a sudden that there is still no one there from Cardiff. Pepsi's here, because he's spending the week with his mum in Shepherd's Bush and Miller's family are here as usual, but no sign of Malik or Lloyd. Maybe Kermit's gone on strike. Yusef waves at me and I wander over to the dock where he says he's got a VO for me if I want to come down to the Scrubs on Saturday.

Then the judges are back and rather than answer Mansfield's request Lord Justice Taylor turns instead to David Elfer and asks if he would care to defend the conduct of the police during these interviews, particularly in the course of Tape 7.

Elfer's response to this is to attempt to shift the goal posts. Rather than defend the police, he opts for bringing in the other evidence against Stephen Miller, corroborating his confession. This consists of an odd pair of statements made by two women who visited Miller in Cardiff Prison.

The two women were Debbie Taylor, Miller's London girlfriend, and Teresa Sidowyk, or 'Auntie Tess', Peggy Farrugia's sister, a woman who had lately befriended the Miller boys and was acting as the family's Cardiff liaison. Mrs Sidowyk volunteered to escort Debbie Taylor to the prison when she came down to Cardiff, and on getting to see Miller she says she asked him point blank if 'he had killed that girl' and he replied that he had not killed her but had been there when it happened – a story which was more or less backed up by Debbie Taylor.

171

Miller, however, denied making such a remark and, with neither Mrs Sidowyk nor Ms Taylor making particularly impressive witnesses, these statements seemed to have played little part in the original trial. Nor does Lord Justice Taylor seem overly impressed by this diversionary tactic, as he returns to his original point: did Mr Elfer agree that the conduct of the police officers in the course of Tape 7 was oppressive?

Cornered, Elfer tries to bluster his way out by arguing that that particular tape may not have been too pleasant, but Miller's solicitor, who was actually there at the time, not just listening to a recording, saw no reason to step in. And, anyway, it wasn't that relevant because he didn't actually confess until later, to the nice police officers.

All very well, says Lord Justice Taylor, but was the conduct oppressive? Yes or no?

Well, says Elfer, in that particular instance perhaps yes, but . . .

Thank you, Mr Elfer, says Lord Justice Taylor.

And suddenly, looking around the court, it seems shocking how isolated Elfer is. Literally, physically isolated. On the defence side, there are three QCs side by side, and behind them two benches full of aides. Elfer is alone on his bench and has just two helpers on the benches behind him, and they too seem remote, heads down, wrapped up in procedure and always just a little too far away from Elfer to pass him anything easily. Today they seem further away than ever and Elfer seems to have ever more trouble going through huge piles of documentation to find the file he needs. And now his face is getting redder and redder as this last exchange seems to break something in him, with its clear confirmation that the judges are not in his corner with him, are cutting him no slack.

Just as the tension is really starting to build, it's lunchtime. Those few of us who are in attendance head over to the pub: myself, Pepsi, and Tony's friend Franca. The pub's even fuller than usual with office workers, it's Thursday and Christmas is a-coming. Me and Pepsi are crammed into a corner next to a 'bloody hell, price of a pint in here' merchant, an old timer outraged by the sight of somebody buying a glass of mineral water. After a while we're let into the big secret, there's a pub in Victoria, just opened up – 99p a pint, mate, that's right, 99 pence. Meanwhile we're scanning the doors for any sign of the Cardiff contingent and starting to envision the embarrassing possibility of the Cardiff Three being set free and nobody there to welcome them out.

No sign by the time we've finished our drinks so I head back over to the court coffee bar. No one there either, except for the *Guardian*'s Duncan Campbell. He's missed the morning session but he's here now and his presence turned out to foreshadow a noticeable swelling of the press ranks when we return upstairs for the afternoon session.

And then it all happens very fast. Elfer is pinned to the wall with Tape 7. Lord Justice Taylor says that he and the other judges were appalled by what they had heard, that it defied belief that police officers would conduct an interview in such a way knowing that they were being recorded and what the demands of PACE are.

At which point the cards are put on the table. PACE is referred to, the section declaring the use of oppressive questioning as being unacceptable and inadmissible. Elfer tries to fall back on the defence that, oppressive questioning or not, the confession was still the truth, but the Law Lords aren't having it. If the behaviour was oppressive – and no one seems to be disputing it – then the confession is out the window. To which Mr Elfer offers the prosecutor's equivalent of putting his hands up and saying, 'It's a fair cop, guv.' Well, he says, more or less, if that's the way you feel, what can I do?

And while this is going on, as if on cue, the doors open and in comes Malik. Then Lloyd. Then Des. Then Kermit. And suddenly there's another recess and we're all standing in the corridor wondering what the hell's happening. Miller must be coming out now. It seems that the crown has thrown in the towel on his case, so surely the others will be free too. Or will they proceed with all the evidence on their individual cases first? Like, what's happening? Malik and Lloyd are just stunned, speechless.

Back inside and Lord Justice Taylor asks Elfer whether he still feels he has a strong case against Paris and Abdullahi. Just for a moment it looks like he's going to make a fight of it. Yes, he says, there is much important evidence against Abdullahi: the testimony of Jacqueline Harris for a start. And as for Tony Paris, well, there's the testimony of Mr Massey.

At which point it is clear that if Elfer hasn't had enough then Justice Popplewell has. At the mention of Massey's name he raises his eyebrows and interjects, 'Ah, the armed robber and self-confessed perjurer.'

And that's it. Elfer can live without having further insult piled on injury. He gathers together what dignity he can and admits that, all things considered, he would not want to continue the case against Paris and Abdullahi. So now we're on the edge of our seats disbelieving that it's all over. And it isn't quite. Next, Lord Justice Taylor invites Paris's and Abdullahi's QCs to add any remarks they choose. So they take it in turns briefly to pour scorn on the notion that the crown had anything at all on their men and to restate their view that the only thing that had convicted them in the first place was Miller's confession, which the jury had wrongly allowed to influence them.

Now it really is all over. Taylor says that he is setting the three free in advance of the full judgment which will follow in due course. So at last we can shout, though even then it's a surprisingly tentative victory cry, still tinged with disbelief. This last half hour has been deeply weird, dreamlike and oddly intangible, like listening to a piece of unfamiliar music. No one's been quite sure where the beat is or where it finishes. The three seemed to be freed half-way through a sentence. We've been waiting for a cue to launch into jubilation, but the whole thing is so low key it never really happens.

Not until the judges have exited, the three have been taken back downstairs, and we're back out in the corridor, does it start to sink in. Malik and Lloyd are crying, Kermit's hugging everyone in sight and everyone else is wearing a dazed stupid grin.

And there are all these people there. Gerry Conlon and Judith Ward have emerged out of nowhere, a guy from the Newham Monitoring Project is busy setting up a press conference, the journalists who were inside are running round like headless chickens playing spot the telephone and moment by moment new journalists are materializing out of the ether. Gradually the whole shebang moves downstairs – apparently the three will be coming out via the cells.

There's a fifteen-minute wait. Lloyd and Malik are besieged by reporters. Word spreads that the press conference will be at the LSE, round the corner. Meanwhile everyone mills about outside the entrance to the cells. The lawyers have come down, looking well chuffed and offering the legal equivalents of 'Over the moon, Brian' to the press. Then there's movement on the far side of the door and we all crowd forward to see the door open. And there they are.

Four years after their arrest, Yusef Abdullahi, Stephen Miller and Tony Paris are back on the street, having had ten minutes to prepare for the experience of being thrust into a mêlée of media folk and well-wishers all pressing claims on their attention. So there they are, trying to juggle tearful family reunions with angry denouncements of British justice for the press.

Stephen and Yusef are looking like the sooner they're out of here the better, and less than enthusiastic at the prospect of a press conference. So it's Tony who takes the brunt of the press assault, and he's in extraordinary form. Words are just pouring out of him. As we start to move off towards the LSE, walking through the Law Courts, Duncan Campbell must have had at most two minutes with him, on the move, and got enough material to publish a full-scale interview in the *Guardian* the next day.

Then we're at the door to the outside, freedom. The second we hit the steps it's bedlam. There's a slew of TV crews waiting, plus a whole bunch of sightseers who've appeared from

God knows where, and in no time it's frightening. The press are fighting to get close but they're being driven back by the determined forward march of the three and their supporters, so they're having to back pedal and this whole knot of twenty or thirty people plus camera equipment looks ready to collapse and crush anybody unfortunate enough to be at the bottom. But a few bellows of anger from the supporters make the press back off a little and we're able to march the hundred yards or so to the LSE.

More milling around and it's set up. We're downstairs in the LSE student union building: the three are sitting on stage, the press are at the front and, behind them, a load of confused students on their way to the snack bar. The students at this erstwhile radical hotbed have less than a clue who these Cardiff Three guys are – 'terrorists or something' – apart from a young black American woman who looks properly aghast at this latest manifestation of British judicial incompetence and racism. Then it's showtime: each of the three has a brother standing behind him and Des, the SWP stalwart, is standing at the back of the stage holding a copy of the *Socialist Worker* in the hope that he'll slip a subliminal plug into the national news (no luck as it goes).

Miller speaks first. He's fired up and angry now, takes the chance to nail the police for their mistreatment of him and goes on to mention some of the others still languishing back in the Scrubs 'the two Tamils, Malcolm Kennedy . . .' And then he stands up. 'That's all,' he says, and exits stage left. Next up is Dullah. Always the most militantly vociferous while in prison, now he looks shell-shocked, and says simply, 'I won't believe it till I see my mother.' So attention moves on to Tony who wraps things up by switching attention to the South Wales police and the evident fact that it's time they found the right man, Mr X or whoever.

Soon it's over. Tony and Yusef leave the stage running off to the cars that'll take them back to Cardiff. The press pack up their gear and hotfoot it back to their newsrooms, the students are left wondering what the hell that was all about and I wander outside into the clear, cold, late afternoon. Outside everyone's talking about the party. It's going to be tonight and it's 'Be there or be square' time.

So six hectic hours after the release of the Three I'm standing in the back bar of the Paddle Steamer. This is unusual enough in itself – it's been years since there was sufficient demand for the Paddle to open both bars – but tonight the place is crammed. It looks like the whole community is packed into the two bars, from kids to old timers. Yusef is over at the bar in the front room with his crew, Tony's in the back with his people, swaying happily amid the rubble of what's evidently already been a hell of a party, John Actie, sporting a skinhead crop and giant baseball jacket, is just leaving and tells us all to follow him up the road to Butetown's new club, Caesar's, where he's organized round two of the night's celebrations. Apparently even Ronnie has been down here, raising a few eyebrows by telling the local TV people how glad he is that all his campaigning has paid off.

Tony and I exchange pleasantries as to what a long strange day it has been and then he swings round, sees me and demands my telephone number. 'You and me are going to make lots of money, see.' Looks like I've been appointed as the official biographer. Then he's carried off again in the swell of well-wishers and after a pint or two of lager it's time to move on down to Caesar's.

Caesar's is down the bottom end of Bute Street, just before the James Street junction. As we approach a cab pulls up, unloading a couple of girls. They're heading into the disco downstairs, while we're directed to the upstairs room. Through the doors the disco is already in full swing: blasting out some reggae tunes, the place is well on the way to getting packed. Things blur, everyone's there. Around one in the morning there's the arrival of a London posse, Satish and the Newham crew. There's a mellow, celebratory mood, drinking and dancing to the revival selection with Kermit at the controls, one and all well blocked up.

Sometime in the night I say to Malik, 'This isn't where Mel's used to be, is it?' And he says 'Yes, this was Mel's, all right. They've just refitted it.'

Last time I was here was twelve years ago. I was nineteen and about to become a redundant printer, rehearsing a band to go busking in Paris and unwittingly setting in motion the events that led me to leave Cardiff and live in London. In Mel's that winter we'd be dancing to Kool and the Gang's 'Celebration' or Lynx's 'You're Lying' or going upstairs to the Roxy Bowie night to dance to 'Ashes to Ashes' or 'The Model' in the company of the cream of Cardiff's hairdressers and art students. And the Docks were still alive then, Spandau Ballet or the Stray Cats playing the Casablanca, r&b bands at the Dowlais every night and another disco upstairs, Blues dances here or there or even in the Community centre. And Lynette White was eleven years old.

'See you at the press conference tomorrow,' was the last thing Malik said as, late in the night but well before the end, I stumbled past him and Alex, entwined like young lovers on Caesar's stairs.

First press conference of the day is at noon at the Marriott Hotel, the former Holiday Inn that was thrown up in the early eighties on the site of the legendary New Moon club. The New Moon was a luridly over-lit hellhole serving bottles of Newkie Brown or nothing, not so much the Hard Rock Café as the Hard Rock dolers canteen, waders essential if you were ever foolish enough to visit the toilets. But, hey! People loved it, it was historical, in a god-awful kind of way. Now it's gone and the Marriott Hotel, much like any other, is its replacement.

When I arrive there's a gaggle of journalists and a TV crew standing around by the entrance. A car's pulling away and it looks like Tony in the front passenger seat. Inside the lobby, Lloyd's there with a couple of people from the campaign. Apparently Tony's gone off to find Yusef and persuade him to come on down and take part. Trouble is, no one's quite sure where Yusef is. Meanwhile the TV crew, from 'Week In,

Week Out', are getting antsy: they've been promised the first exclusive interviews and they've got a 'special' scheduled for this evening.

After a while the rival journalists are dispersed, told to come to Caesar's at four, and the rest of us head up to a suite the TV people have booked. We sit around for a while eating BBC sandwiches and watching the TV folk attempt to maintain their professional calm. Then Tony arrives but no Yusef. More sandwiches, cups of tea, Tony ruling the roost. Lloyd causes further aggravation by demanding cheese sandwiches that have not shared a plate with ham. Still no Yusef, tempers starting to fray. Tea's not enough so out comes the booze, bottles of Grolsch mostly, brandy for Tony. After a while more of this, I've had enough, say I'll be down at Caesar's later.

So I get there late but there's nothing happening at all and eventually I wind up round at Malik's. He and Alex are cooling out in the living room, waiting for 'Week In, Week Out'. Turns out Yusef did show up but not till five or so, so the TV went ahead but the Caesar's press conference had to be blown out. So we watch the documentary and it's fine but already somehow it's over. The party was last night, there's time for a rest this evening but tomorrow life's going to have to go on.

And Malik's still got his own relatively petty but still aggravating problems with the police to sort out. They're still looking to charge him with assault, after an altercation with a screw in the police cells, following his last arrest. And Yusef's already driving Malik crazy. Plus he's back with Jackie, went back there last night. There's just a slight sense that Yusef's out and that's great, but his suffering has been seen by everyone and he should at least receive some compensation (though how little and how late remains to be seen) but Malik and Alex have had their lives stood on their heads for years. It has cost them dear too.

A couple of weeks later, just into the New Year, it's lunchtime and I'm standing in the bar of the Paddle Steamer. Everything's back to normal in the Paddle: there's just a few old folk scattered around in front of the TV bellowing the answers to one of the terminally inane quiz shows that clutter up the airwaves at this time of day. I'm here with Lloyd and we've just popped in to phone Tony, who's back living with his missus round the corner, to see if he wants to meet us down here.

But no, Tony wants us to come up, which doesn't please Lloyd too much as he and Denise, Tony's wife, don't get on too brilliantly. So once we're installed in Tony's kitchen, a couple of storeys up in one of the Hodges Square low-rise blocks, Lloyd makes a speedy exit and leaves us to it. Tony's listening to music and helping Denise get the dinner sorted out. He talks about the support he's had from his family, from his wife and from his brother and sister and how they kept him strong, and how hard it's been to be away from his little boy, who's spent most of his life so far with his daddy in prison for murder.

Tony's got to go shopping and pick his boy up from school so we agree to talk later. But when we do sit down later, while Tony eats his tea, the first thing he wants to talk is business. He still hasn't had any compensation money, no interim payment, no nothing and his family is hurting, so can I get him some money for doing this interview? I say I'll try, but explain the facts of life, that writing this book isn't making me rich, rather the reverse, if anything. So we go ahead with the interview but neither my heart nor Tony's is in it, and he's so concerned that what he says might be valuable that he avoids saying almost anything of interest and I wonder if Truman Capote ever had this kind of trouble. Still, we agree to meet up next day and see some people, get a picture of his life and his people.

We have the interview and mostly what I'm left with is some kind of composite memory of talking to some guy who's ready to change the world because changing the life he's leading within these four walls looks impossible. There are times when I just feel that 'Yes, there is a cycle of deprivation' as I watch another infant struggling to fit *Hellraiser 2* or, yes, clichéd but true, *Silence of the Lambs*, into the video recorder in between practising his kickboxing and getting shouted at by everyone, shouted at over the noise of the fighting on the TV screen and the baby crying in the next room and the reggae tapes playing in the kitchen where the kid's mother is willing the tranquillizers to kick in and fast looking older than her man who has nothing more to worry about than changing the world.

And by the time Tony and I parted, after a fruitless search for Dullah involving a visit to Pauline Abdullahi's place down at the bottom, round the corner from the Windsor Esplanade, we've ended up having a bull-headed row about whether the building we could see across the water was Llandough Hospital or not. By that time we've each had about enough.

Epilogue

Five years after the lonesome death of Lynette White, we are no closer to knowing who killed her. All that can be said with any certainty is that the death of this woman, whose life was characterized mostly by the lack of attention paid to her, has sown a bitter harvest, left its mark on too many lives.

There have been the obvious costs: the four years of their lives lost by Tony Paris, Yusef Abdullahi and Stephen Miller. The suffering of their families and, in Tony's and Yusef's cases, their children. The two years spent in prison by John and Ronnie Actie only to be found not guilty (and it remains unbelievable that a legal system that can facilitate £500,000 payments for the most paltry of libels may not offer anything to these two men who were branded as murderers, locked up for two years, and still walk under a cloud).

The suffering of their families is another obvious debit. Also the suffering of Lynette White's family. Not only seeing their daughter dehumanized throughout the media as 'the prostitute Lynette White', but then to be given the false comfort of having the wrong people blamed for her murder. Their suffering will never be compensated nor even lessened until the real killer is found. The millions of pounds of public money wasted on the trials, the imprisonment, the appeal and the eventual compensation. The lives wrecked in the course of the investigation itself. In particular the lives of the so-called witnesses who were coerced into testifying – Leanne Vilday, Angela Psaila, Mark Grommek and Paul Atkins – all of these have had their lives blighted by this affair. The unpaid efforts of those who campaigned against the injustice of the original verdict, whether family members like Malik, Alex and Lloyd,

Butetown people like Kermit and Pepsi and Keith Morell, or concerned outsiders like the redoubtable investigator Satish Sekar.

But there have also been less obvious costs. The blow to the standing of the South Wales Police Force in general and the Butetown police in particular. Following as it did on the heels of the appalling case of the Darvell brothers (cynically framed by the Swansea police for the murder of a sex-shop manageress), the acquittal of the Cardiff Three leaves a lasting stain.

The reputation of the local media was also damaged. The local Thomson group papers, the *Western Mail* and particularly the *South Wales Echo* were craven in their parroting of the police line on the case and gave short shrift to the defence campaign right up until the very last moment. This exposes the extent to which short-staffed local papers have become complacently reliant on the police to provide them with their crime coverage, ready wrapped in nice little packages.

Another cost was the loss of respect for the local politicians who signally failed to protest at the miscarriage of justice, whether national figures, like the MP Alun Michael, or local, like Councillor Betty Campbell. Mr Michael, in the run-up to election year, showed a pusillanimous unwillingness to involve himself, presumably for fear that he might get his spotless Kinnockite hands dirty. Councillor Campbell should have known better; her job must be to represent all those in her community, including those with less than savoury reputations.

And then, too, in some ways this case has been accursed. The first judge died during the trial (which may have been a relief for the Acties at least, the legal whisper being that the good judge was firmly of a mind that all five were guilty), the conviction coincided with the deposing of Margaret Thatcher, and the acquittal with the separation of Charles and Di. Two suspects died in the course of the investigation: first, Martin Tucker, from a heroin overdose that surprised few who knew him, the second, Tony Brace, more bizarrely, run over when walking in the middle of the road, heading the wrong way up a slip road somewhere near Taff's Well. And finally Tony's father, the seaman from Nevis, died a saddened man just weeks before his son was freed from prison.

And somewhere out there is the killer.

Mr X still seems the prime candidate, this man whose combination of rare blood group, psychological profile, criminal record and association with Lynette White made him such a convincing suspect. The police, however, are still sticking with their assertion that the DNA tests ruled him out. This would be fine if there were not some lurking doubt as to how authoritative the DNA tests can have been in this case, given that there was only a very partial sample lifted from the blood in the murder room.

The other, still more ominous, theory is that there might be a connection with the Geraldine Polk case. Geraldine Polk was a young woman from the west Cardiff suburb of Fairwater who was found dead on 22 December 1990, just a month after the conviction of the Cardiff Three. Like Lynette she had died from multiple stab wounds, eighty-five of them in this case. Her killer has never been found, but the police ruled out any connection with the Lynette White murder. After all, they had the guilty men in prison. Didn't they?

As far as the South Wales police are concerned this, of course, must be the nightmare scenario – that these two killings could be the work of one man who might, presumably, strike again. Either way, their stated policy of not actively pursuing the Lynette White murder case looks dangerously complacent. And arrogant, going on insulting too.

But there may be good things that will come out of it all. The success of a campaign started by a handful of relatives, without the first idea of what they were meant to be doing, must be an inspiration to the countless others who do daily battle with injustice. And so it may just be that the people of Butetown may find the strength and self-belief to ensure that this Bay Development that has threatened to engulf them may instead be made to work for their benefit too.

And in that respect the watchwords for the people of Butetown should be those that Tony Paris uttered immediately
after being set free: 'They wanted anybody for that murder.
They thought we were anybodies but we were somebodies.'

It's 1 April 1993 and two years since I started writing this
book. And even then that was not the start of it. I remember
how it started: I was reading the paper early in 1989 and there
was a story about this murder in Wales, five men had been
arrested for murdering a prostitute and the two main prosecution witnesses were fellow prostitutes who had, apparently,
been forced to join in the killing to ensure their silence. The
kicker, as far as I was concerned, was that this murder had
happened in Butetown.

I couldn't believe it. It sounded extraordinary: like a plot
from a penny dreadful, it seemed hardly credible that real life
could work out like that, but still . . . I couldn't believe it
because it was too perfect. For a long time I'd wanted to write
about Butetown, the black-sheep neighbourhood of my home
town, and this looked like the ideal excuse. So maybe that
would be a better way of putting it, this book didn't start with
the murder of Lynette White at all, truer to say it started
when I was seventeen and ventured down to the Docks for
the first time and discovered just what went on behind the
green door. I knew then that I was in the midst of a hidden
history that needed telling.

I didn't do much about it at first. I was in the middle of
planning my first book. I went to the States that spring to
travel for a couple of months researching that book. But, before
I left, I sent an outline for an article to a magazine I wrote
for. When I came back I found that the magazine weren't
keen to commission anything on a case that was still *sub judice*
and, as it transpired, was to remain *sub judice* for a long time
yet. But the case still preyed on my mind and when I made
trips back home to Cardiff I would mention the case to people,
see if they knew anything.

The response was remarkable. Remarkable, first, in that

almost everyone I knew seemed to know something, and second, in that what they knew worried them, or scared them, made them look around the pub to see who was listening, made them shut up, or walk away from the table, made them go weird.

It was a weird time in the city. There was some bad cocaine business going on around town, everyone seemed sure of that, seemed sure there was some kind of battle going on with interloping Yardies. People were showing up in pubs with shotguns, a lot of people had stories about that kind of thing. And then one of the guys arrested was a man called John Actie and everyone seemed to have a story about him, not that most of them knew him personally, you understand. Big bad John, they said. Bad news, they said. And the whisper was that he may be locked up inside but his family was on the outside and looking out for him. No witness is safe, they said. I'd keep out of that business, they said. After all, a mate of my mate's moved to the States to get away from it all, that's the kind of thing, they said.

So I did what any dedicated investigative reporter type would do. I said to myself, 'All right, I'll write it as a novel.' There were other reasons too for this decision. For already I had my own agenda, my own ideas about what might have happened. What I wanted to have happened, I suppose.

Thirty yards from where Lynette died, they'd pulled down a place called the Mount Stuart in the name of redevelopment. No one seemed to mind too much since it was only an old pub that no one much went into any more, but to me, apart from the fact that it was anyway a quite beautiful Victorian boozer, it was also a living, breathing reminder of the old Docks. I can't rationally explain why, I doubt if I drank in there more than a dozen times, but I loved the place. And the redevelopment killed it, removed it to make way for a bridge that is never ever going to be built. The Mount Stuart died pointlessly and unlamented, and I wanted to see the death of this Lynette White as part of that same process. I wanted there to be a link between the faceless bastards who pulled down my Mount Stuart and the one (or ones) that killed this girl. I wanted to say that there are forces at work in this city that care nothing for history or young lives. I wanted to say that this is a tainted town. I wanted to write a novel that would point the finger at the 'Labour Party' oligarchy.

So I started to write a novel, which was OK as far as it went. That is to say, as long as I was writing about what I knew it went pretty well, but once I got on to the Butetown side of the story I wanted to tell, I realized that it was not working. I had been to Butetown, I was intrigued by Butetown, but I did not remotely know nor understand Butetown. And I could not fictionalize it without repeating all the usual clichés or writing about it as if it were just the same as a familiar part of London, a Dalston or a Kensal Rise. All of which need not, of course, have been a barrier to writing fiction, I could just have made it up, but that wasn't what I wanted, I wanted to try to get Butetown right. So I got stuck.

The strength in writing a novel was that I could build up my conspiracy. My fictional Lynette – whom I called, and this is genuinely weird as I'd never heard of Ms Vilday at this point, Leanne – was not 'just a prostitute', she was a smart girl who'd had a hard upbringing and had started hustling out of a kind of bloody-minded self-sufficiency shot through with a deathwish.

This Lynette who – and I suppose this is some kind of illustration of the fact that this death did strike some kind of a communal chord – was a projection of the worst that might have happened to a woman or rather two women that I had known when I still lived in Cardiff, inasmuch as they lived lives without safety nets and were perhaps cursed with a prettiness that allowed them to drift through life in the certain knowledge that there would always be someone to buy the next drink. This Lynette had acquired knowledge from her work, knowledge of some civic scam connected to the Bay Development. She tried to turn that knowledge into profit and ended up dead – pretty much your typical modern urban thriller plot.

That's the way I wanted to see things, but, as I say, I got stuck. Then I got a call from a novelist I know and he asked if I would be interested in co-writing a true-crime book about this case that he'd recently heard about, this murder case in Cardiff . . . And at first I thought, 'No, I'm writing my novel', but then I thought, 'Why not? I need to know more.' So I said yes.

The collaboration never worked out and what started out a quick, straightforward book instead sucked me in, took me two years to make any sense of.

When it did start to make sense I had to accept that my conspiracy couldn't hold. The way I wanted to see things was not the way things actually work. For a start Lynette White was a hustler, pure and simple, and she was murdered, I am sure, by a sexual psychopath, not for any ulterior motive (though it has to be said that my idea was probably more plausible than the police's fantasy of a murder by five men, all locked into a vow of silence – a plot too stupid for even the lamest pulp fiction).

But I still wanted a conspiracy. If Lynette's murder was simply a random horror, then surely, I figured, some planning must have gone into the eventual arrests. What I would have been happy to prove would have been that the Cardiff Bay Development Corporation had explicitly pressurized the police into making the arrests to clear up this unsightly and unsolved case.

Well, I cannot believe that this was the case either. But perhaps only because there was no need for it to be the case. I suspect that at the higher levels of the CBDC, the police and the local political establishment, the people who run things know each other. And they know each other's concerns. There would simply be no need for a CBDC exec to tell a Chief Constable that the CBDC was concerned about this murder. It would be obvious.

My belief is that the police appreciated that it would be politically expedient to clear up this case. So, in some ways the police and I were in the same boat, the good ship conspiracy. We both had our agendas, our visions of how this story could be tied up into a nice little package. Me, I wanted a good story, a *story-like story*. And who could blame them for being tempted. After all, finding a sex killer in the general population is needle-in-a-haystack time. The sorry truth is that the police are not very good at solving crimes that are not committed by career villains. That's to say, if there's a professionally executed armed robbery, the police will know where to start looking and, sooner or later, someone will grass up those responsible. But sex killers don't go round in packs, they don't drink in villains' pubs; they are, as the cliché goes, just like you or me or the next-door neighbour.

The other sorry truth is that writing a book, this book, isn't going to make life better for Butetown. Tiger Bay will not be rebuilt in a day. The book didn't get the boys out of jail and it won't rebuild their lives. It's just a book.

And for Lynette White it's too late anyway. And what she needed was not a book but . . . love, most probably.

☐	UNLAWFUL CARNAL KNOWLEDGE Wendy Holden	0-00-638258-4	£5.99
☐	DEADLIER THAN THE MALE Alix Kirsta	0-00-637849-8	£5.99
☐	LIFE'S DOMINION Ronald Dworkin	0-00-686309-4	£7.99
☐	SEXING THE MILLENNIUM Linda Grant	0-00-637768-8	£7.99

These books are available from your local bookseller or can be ordered direct from the publishers.

To order direct just tick the titles you want and fill in the form below:

Name: _____

Address: _____

_____

Postcode: _____

Send to: HarperCollins Mail Order, Dept 8, HarperCollins*Publishers*, Westerhill Road, Bishopbriggs, Glasgow G64 2QT.

Please enclose a cheque or postal order or your authority to debit your Visa/Access account –

Credit card no: _____

Expiry date: _____

Signature: _____

– to the value of the cover price plus:

UK & BFPO: Add £1.00 for the first and 25p for each additional book ordered.

Overseas orders including Eire, please add £2.95 service charge.

Books will be sent by surface mail but quotes for airmail despatches will be given on request.

24 HOUR TELEPHONE ORDERING SERVICE FOR
ACCESS/VISA CARDHOLDERS –
TEL: GLASGOW 041-772 2281 or LONDON 081-307 4052